CROSSWAY BOOKS
BY STEPHEN F. OLFORD

Not I, But Christ
The Way of Holiness

THE WAY
of
HOLINESS

Signposts to Guide Us

STEPHEN F. OLFORD

CROSSWAY BOOKS • WHEATON, ILLINOIS
A DIVISION OF GOOD NEWS PUBLISHERS

Library of Congress Cataloging-in-Publication Data
Olford, Stephen F.
   The way of holiness : signposts to guide us / Stephen F. Olford.
      p.   cm.
   Includes bibliographical references and Index.
   1. Christian life.   2. Devil.   I. Title.
BV4501.2.0463 1998   248.4—DC21   97-29012
   ISBN 0-89107-977-7

06	05	04	03	02	01	00	99	98
15	14	13	12	11	10	9	8	7	6	5	4	3	2	1

I dedicate this volume to
those who are determined to walk
"the Highway of Holiness." ISAIAH 35:8

CONTENTS

FOREWORD

The Way of Holiness describes the walk of faith and obedience in the life of progressive sanctification made possible in us by the Holy Spirit through obedience to the Word of God. In a time when so much preaching and teaching is limited to topical subjects—often unrelated to a biblical context—it is refreshing to have a series of expositions scripturally and simply unfolded to lead us "in Christ's triumphal procession" (2 Cor. 2:14 REB). Such teaching is the "signature" of Stephen Olford! Thousands around the world have shared the liberating experience that he expounds in this book.

The life and message of this beloved servant of God have stirred my heart and challenged my own commitment to a life of holiness. You cannot hear him or read his works without experiencing a fresh new confrontation with the lordship of Jesus Christ. He is indeed a modern-day prophet.

For over one hundred years the Keswick movement has proclaimed the truth that every Christian can live a life of victory in the Lord Jesus Christ. The early leaders described this truth by different names and terms, but semantics must never rob us of what is clear and consistent in the Holy Scriptures.

Following the principles of this book will lead you along the way of holiness that God has predestined for all of us.

CHARLES F. STANLEY

ACKNOWLEDGMENTS

The chapters in this book are the finished product of messages delivered extemporaneously to audiences around the world and in the churches I have served. In the "flow" of such preaching, many quotes, concepts, and illustrations were brought to mind without specific documentation. I, therefore, acknowledge all sources of such material—heard or read—from the "gifts of men" (Eph. 4:8) with which our risen Lord has enriched the church.

I also acknowledge with gratitude the efforts and efficiency of those involved in the preparation of this book. I single out especially Anita Bosley, my computist; Jennifer Balmer, my projects assistant; and Victoria Kuhl, my homiletical secretary.

Then I must say a heartfelt thank you to my very dear friend and colleague Dr. Charles Stanley for his gracious foreword to this book. Having shared church pulpits and conference ministry with him on many occasions, I know that we are "on the same page" in our understanding of God's purpose for His people in the "enfolding drama of redemption." He, like myself, has entered into deeper experiences of that divine purpose by walking the way of holiness in the power of the Holy Spirit. Once again—thank you, Charles.

INTRODUCTION

As you therefore have received
Christ Jesus the Lord, so walk in Him.
COLOSSIANS 2:6

God has called every Christian to walk the "Highway of Holiness" (Isa. 35:8). To guide us along the way, He has provided "signposts." Each one is important and precipitates a crisis of decision if we would move on in God's purpose of progressive sanctification.

Perhaps the best verse in the New Testament to illustrate this principle is found in Colossians 2:6. It reads, "As you therefore have received Christ Jesus the Lord, so *walk* in Him." The connective "therefore" looks back to the apostle Paul's previous statement about the stable faith of the Colossian believers (v. 5). He then states that the crisis that initially brought them to the acceptance of the Gospel is to *be a pattern* of their continuing faithfulness. Three crises are implied in this verse and set the pattern of our Christian life—until we see Jesus face to face.

THE CRISIS OF DECISION

"As you therefore have *received* Christ Jesus the Lord" (v. 6). There came a point in time when these Colossians decided to follow Jesus. Drawn by the prevenient workings of the Spirit, they

accepted Christ. In a very real sense, we reaffirm that initial decision every day of our lives.

THE CRISIS OF DEVOTION

"As you therefore have received Christ Jesus the *Lord*" (v. 6).
Vincent, in his *Word Studies in the New Testament*,[1] points out
that the Greek emphasizes here the saving *lordship* of Christ.
The text reads, "As you have received *the* Christ, even Jesus,
the Lord." There was no "easy believism" in Paul's presenta-
tion of the Gospel. *Decision* was to be accompanied and followed by *devotion*. Jesus Christ *is* Lord and, therefore, *must* be
Lord in our lives.

THE CRISIS OF DIRECTION

"As you therefore have received Christ Jesus the Lord, *so walk in
Him*" (v. 6). The Colossians were to walk in dependence on
Christ and by the direction of Christ. Walking speaks of the normal pattern of living. It suggests the steady progress of the one
who patiently, but persistently, goes on in the face of temptation
and opposition, giving heed to every biblical signpost along the
Highway of Holiness.

So there are crises in the Christian life, and each one is to be
faced with a step of decision, a stride of devotion, and a sense of
direction. We shall consider some of these signposts that the
Christian must face as he walks the pathway to glory. John
Sammis (1846–1919) must have had this "walk" in mind when
he wrote:

Signposts to Guide Us

When we walk with the Lord
In the light of His Word,
What a glory He sheds on our way!
While we do His good will
He abides with us still,
And with all who will trust and obey.
Trust and obey—
For there's no other way
To be happy in Jesus
But to trust and obey.

The Signpost of
SINFULNESS

✳

Come now, you who say, "Today or tomorrow we will go to such and such a city, spend a year there, buy and sell, and make a profit"; whereas you do not know what will happen tomorrow. For what is your life? It is even a vapor that appears for a little time and then vanishes away. Instead you ought to say, "If the Lord wills, we shall live and do this or that." But now you boast in your arrogance. All such boasting is evil. Therefore, to him who knows to do good and does not do it, to him it is sin.

JAMES 4:13-17

✳

I say then: Walk in the Spirit, and you shall not fulfill the lust of the flesh. For the flesh lusts against the Spirit, and the Spirit against the flesh; and these are contrary to one another, so that you do not do the things that you wish. But if you are led by the Spirit, you are not under the law. Now the works of the flesh are evident, which are: adultery, fornication, uncleanness, lewdness, idolatry, sorcery, hatred, contentions, jealousies, outbursts of wrath, selfish ambitions, dissensions, heresies, envy, murders, drunkenness, revelries, and the like;

of which I tell you beforehand, just as I also told you in time past, that those who practice such things will not inherit the kingdom of God. But the fruit of the Spirit is love, joy, peace, longsuffering, kindness, goodness, faithfulness, gentleness, self-control. Against such there is no law.

GALATIANS 5:16-23

The Signpost of
SINFULNESS

One of the misleading half-truths that preachers can convey to babes in Christ is the notion that after conversion there are no more temptations, testings, or failings. It therefore comes as a great shock when a young believer discovers that it is still possible for him or her to sin. It is the crisis of failure in the Christian's walk. Of course, "there's victory in Jesus"; but there can also be defeat when we cease to abide in Him. John the apostle reminds us that "if we say that we have not sinned, we make Him [God] a liar, and His word is not in us" (1 John 1:10).

This signpost of sin is highlighted in the passages quoted at the beginning of the chapter, and I want to deal with the subject from a threefold aspect: the mystery of sin, the misery of sin, and the mastery of sin in the believer's life.

THE MYSTERY OF SIN IN THE BELIEVER'S LIFE

"To him who knows to do good and does not do it, to him it is sin" (James 4:17). Although this verse can be applied to the unregenerate, its primary message is to believers. James has referred already to believers as "doers of the word, and not hearers only" (James 1:22)—those who have received "the implanted word" (James 1:21).

At the same time, there is a mysterious "moral dualism" in

our text. Here we have "good" and "sin" in the same person. When we search for the explanation, we find it in the Word of God. In the fifth chapter of Galatians, verses 16-18, Paul writes, "I say then: Walk in the Spirit, and you shall not fulfill the lust of the flesh. For the flesh lusts against the Spirit, and the Spirit against the flesh; and these are contrary to one another, so that you do not do the things that you wish. But if you are led by the Spirit, you are not under the law." Here is the mystery of moral dualism.

A Moral Dualism That
Polarizes the Believer's Life

"For the flesh lusts against the Spirit, and the Spirit against the flesh; and these are contrary to one another" (Gal. 5:17). Have you ever experienced that tug-of-war in your life—a desire to please God and yet a desire to please self? Here Paul contrasts the self-centered life with the Spirit-centered life and shows that these are contrary to one another. "To will is present with me, but how to perform what is good I do not find" (Rom. 7:18). Therefore, "To him who knows to do good and does not do it, to him it is sin" (James 4:17). Look first at:

☐ THE SELF-CENTERED LIFE

"The works of the flesh are evident" (Gal. 5:19). Although those who commit such sins are not worthy to inherit the kingdom of God, we all know that each of us has the potential to commit these sins.

☐ *There Are the Sexual Sins.* "Adultery, fornication, uncleanness, lewdness" (Gal. 5:19). Charles Colson, in his book *The Body*, states that "the divorce rate among the clergy is increasing faster than in any other profession. Numbers show that one in ten have had an affair with a member of their congregation, and 25 percent have had illicit sexual contact."[1] Our country is in the grip of sexual sins, and if the illustrious historian Arnold Toynbee is right, this is one of the evidences of a degenerate society and a decadent church.

☐ *There Are the Spiritual Sins.* "Idolatry, sorcery" (Gal. 5:20). Idolatry means anything or anyone who comes between God and yourself, thereby becoming the center of your affection and attention. God has condemned it! Sorcery or witchcraft literally means drug-taking—the very situation we're in today—and this "drug-taking" is invading the church of Jesus Christ. What Aldous Huxley and others predicted has come to pass. People are seeking religious experiences through "kicks" of all kinds, and this is wrapped up in the occultism we see around us. Through the New Age movement and other devices, Satan is on his last rampage before Jesus Christ comes back again. I don't remember any time in my life when I've sensed such demonic oppression!

And we could go on. We see "hatred, contentions, jealousies, outbursts of wrath, selfish ambitions, dissensions, heresies" (or parties into which divisions crystallize) (Gal. 5:20; 1 Cor. 11:19), and all this within the realm of our religious life.

☐ *There Are the Social Sins.* "Envy . . . drunkenness, revelries" (Gal. 5:21). All these sins can be found in my heart and in your heart, unless we know what it is to be protected by the blood of Christ and by the power of the Spirit. Paul is not talking about an *act* of sin, but the *habit* of sin. The fact that the believer is not under law but under grace is no excuse for sin. If anything, it is an encouragement to live in victory. Our text still applies: "To him who knows to do good and does not do it, to him it is sin" (James 4:17).

The Signpost of Sinfulness

But then there is:

☐ THE SPIRIT-CENTERED LIFE

"The fruit of the Spirit is love, joy, peace, longsuffering, kindness, goodness, faithfulness, gentleness, self-control. Against such there is no law" (Gal. 5:22-23). Here is a nine-dimensional configuration of the life of Christ. It interprets the greatest commandment to be found anywhere in Scripture, namely, "You shall love the LORD your God with all your heart, with all your soul, with all your strength, and with all your mind [that's our relationship Godward], and your neighbor as yourself [that's our relationship manward]" (Luke 10:27). The self-centered life is diametrically opposed to the Spirit-centered life.

But I want to go further and point out that the mystery of sin is not only moral dualism that polarizes the believer's life, but also:

A Moral Dualism That
Paralyzes the Believer's Life
"The flesh lusts against the Spirit, and the Spirit against the flesh; and these are contrary to one another, so that you do not do the things that you wish" (Gal. 5:17). Christians know very well that their responsibility is to witness to Jesus every day. Countless opportunities present themselves to say a word for Christ, but they don't do it. Most of us know that the only life that counts for God is a life that starts each day in a quiet place with a definite time, a specific plan, and an expectant spirit to wait on God to speak; yet we don't have our quiet times. Our commitment is to be at the prayer meeting every week, knowing that the church only moves forward on its knees; yet we don't go to the prayer meetings.

Signposts to Guide Us

Do we know why that is? I'll tell you. Not only have we a polarized life, but a paralyzed life—that inner contradiction, that mystery of sin in the believer's life. And we are never going to be triumphant in our Christian experience until we learn to gain victory over the mystery of sin. Where this mystery is unresolved there is:

THE MISERY OF SIN IN THE BELIEVER'S LIFE

"To him who knows to do good and does not do it, to him it is sin" (James 4:17). In this chapter of James, we have three aspects of this misery of sin described for us.

The Misery of a Worldly Life

God asks, "Do you not know that friendship with the world is enmity with God? Whoever therefore wants to be a friend of the world makes himself an enemy of God" (v. 4). In verse 13 James chides those who say, "Come now, you who say, 'Today or tomorrow we will go to such and such a city, spend a year there, buy and sell, and make a profit.'" Someone asks, "What's wrong with that? What's wrong with planning? What's wrong with traveling? What's wrong with selling? What's wrong with buying? What's wrong with getting rich?" Nothing—except that you do it without God. For a Christian to launch out on any project without God is to become worldly. Worldliness in Scripture means carnal affections, carnal attractions, and carnal ambitions (see 1 John 2:13-17). We are living in an hour when we're so brainwashed by television, radio, the press, and even by some preachers that we are made to feel out of it—unless we are "with it" in the world.

The Signpost of Sinfulness

Vance Havner tells the story of the time he and a friend visited New York City. They toured Rockefeller Center and other famous buildings. They went around Manhattan on a boat. They browsed in shops. At the end of the day, Dr. Havner was completely worn out. When the country preacher was asked what he thought of New York, he replied, "Well, I haven't seen anything I can't live without!"

Paul writes, "I beseech you therefore, brethren, by the mercies of God, that you present your bodies a living sacrifice, holy, acceptable to God, which is your reasonable service. And do not be conformed to this world, but be transformed by the renewing of your mind" (Rom. 12:1-2). J. B. Phillips renders it, "Don't let the world around you squeeze you into its own mold." Revival will only come when a remnant of God's people are as distinct from the world as Jesus was. He ate and drank with sinners, but He was "holy, harmless, undefiled, separate from sinners" (Heb. 7:26). Can you be marked out in any company as a clear-cut Christian? In your plans, which may be all legitimate, does God have first place?

The Misery of a Wasteful Life

"You do not know what will happen tomorrow. For what is your life? It is even a vapor that appears for a little time and then vanishes away" (v. 14). James is really asking, "What is the nature of your life? How long do you have to fulfill your destiny? Don't you know that your life is as a vapor?" In the morning the mist hangs heavily upon the trees, but presently the sun comes up, and before you know it, the mist has disappeared. That's a picture of your life.

Speaking from personal experience, I've had three crises that have impressed the brevity of life upon me. The first was on a deathbed, at the age of twenty-one, when God broke into my life through a letter from my father in which he quoted this couplet:

> *Only one life, 'twill soon be past,*
> *Only what's done for Christ will last.*

Those words shattered me! My wasteful life, up until that point, had to be reviewed in the presence of God. And blessed be His name, He not only forgave me, but He healed me! The second crisis was in 1948 at Mayo Clinic when I was given a slim chance of recovery from serious surgery. The third crisis came after fourteen wonderful years of ministry at Calvary Baptist Church in New York City, when, in the very throes and thrills of preaching, I was suddenly afflicted with something that rendered me useless for seven months.

Oh, you may talk about your strength today, but tomorrow you may be as helpless as a baby. You can't guarantee a single day. For whom are you living? What is the destiny of your life? Nothing is more miserable than to know you are living a wasteful life. One day you are going to stand before the judgment seat of Christ, and if your life has been self-centered, worldly, manifesting those sexual, spiritual, and social sins we've been thinking about, you are going to see that whole life of yours burned up. You will have the unutterable shame of pressing the charred embers of a wasted life into His pierced hands and saying, "That's all I have for You, Lord."

The Misery of a Willful Life

James says, "But now you boast in your arrogance. All such boasting is evil" (4:16). If you continue in a worldly life, a wasteful life, you will soon discover yourself in a willful state where you couldn't care less. I have talked to preachers and to Christians generally who have become so careless and callous that they joke and boast about their subnormal Christian living. Such individuals are on a collision course, for "to him who knows to do good and does not do it, to him it is sin" (v. 17).

But, thank God, there is an answer.

THE MASTERY OF SIN IN THE BELIEVER'S LIFE

"You ought to say, 'If the Lord wills, we shall live and do this or that'" (v. 15). The mastery of sin in the believer's life has a twofold solution:

Recognition of the Divine Will

"You ought to say, 'If the Lord wills'" (v. 15). I am still mindful of those letters I used to receive from a generation past where I rarely read through many lines from a Christian without seeing the initials D.V.—*Deo volente*—"if the Lord wills."

We have to recognize that this universe is governed by a sovereign God who is and lives and rules and cares. God is still on the throne, and He has a will not only in the material but in the moral realm as well. In fact, you cannot pray the Lord's Prayer without recognizing the will of God; and your life cannot be victorious, pure, or fruitful outside of that will. God has a will for your life. He proved it once and for all by giving His Son to the death of the cross that you might be saved and sanctified. "*This is the will of God, your sanctification*" (1 Thess. 4:3).

Signposts to Guide Us

Resignation to the Divine Will

"'If the Lord wills, we shall live and do this or that'" (v. 15). It is one thing to recognize the will of God; it is another thing to surrender to it. The passage in the Word of God that helps us understand God's will is Romans 12:1-2, where Paul links the life of surrender to the knowledge of that "good and acceptable and perfect will of God."

☐ GOD'S WILL IS PROFITABLE FOR YOUR LIFE

"That you may prove what is that *good* . . . will of God" (Rom. 12:2). Now "to him who knows to do good and does not do it, to him it is sin" (James 4:17). Here is the will of God that you cannot afford to neglect, ignore, or disobey—because it is *good.* Think of all the synonyms bound up in that word *good,* because all that is good is in the will of God.

I recall a nurse who broke down one Sunday morning at Calvary Baptist Church, New York City, under the power and conviction of the Holy Spirit. After the service I sat alongside her and asked if I could be of help. She explained her problem: "I want to yield my life to God. I want Him to have everything, but I'm afraid God will take mean advantage of me." She was talking right out of her heart! Turning to Romans 12:1-2, I showed her that God's will is *good.* She celebrated a victory that Sunday morning!

☐ GOD'S WILL IS PLEASURABLE FOR YOUR LIFE

"That you may prove what is that . . . *acceptable* . . . will of God" (Rom. 12:2). It is "the sweet will of God." There is no place in heaven or earth more delightful or more enjoyable than the center of God's will. And whether you're serving the Lord as a missionary on some remote island, or whether you're in a very difficult home situation with belligerent parents, you can still be happy if you're in the will of God.

☐ GOD'S WILL IS PURPOSEFUL FOR YOUR LIFE

"That you may prove what is that . . . *perfect* will of God" (Rom. 12:2). That word denotes an unfolding drama, not only experientially now, but eschatologically in a day to come. If you and I are in the center of God's will, He is not only going to condition and conform us to His image moment by moment, day by day, but He is going to bring us into all the fullness of His ultimate purpose in that eternal state.

Study the life of the Lord Jesus, and you will discover that the one consuming passion of His life was the will of God. He looked into the face of His earthly parents and said, "Did you not know that I must be about My Father's business?" (Luke 2:49). That was submission to the will of God as the *Son*.

At the height of His ministry, as He led a sinful woman at the well of Sychar to the fountain of living water, He could say to His disciples (who seemed more interested in sandwiches than in soul-winning), "My food is to do the will of Him who sent Me, and to finish His work" (John 4:34). This was submission to the will of God as a *Servant*.

Then in the garden of Gethsemane, wrestling with the great problem of being made sin for the human race, He prayed, "Father, if it is possible, let this cup pass from Me; nevertheless, not as I will, but as You will" (Matt. 26:39). That was submission to the will of God as *Savior*. When Jesus prayed that prayer in the garden, He mastered sin forever, for that was the prelude to

Calvary where He would cry, "Finished!" (John 19:30) and where He gained a victory that you and I can know in our lives.

When you surrender like that, something happens. The Bible says that God gives the Holy Spirit "to those who obey Him" (Acts 5:32). The verb *obey* is the same as in verse 29 where Peter says, "We ought to obey God rather than men." The word implies obedience to an appointed authority. So we need the mighty Spirit of God to strengthen us to do the will of God, just as Jesus was strengthened by that angel in the garden of Gethsemane (Luke 22:43). You can pray all night, all day, all month, and all year for the enabling of the Holy Spirit, but your request will never be realized until you are prepared to do the will of God.

We have thought about the mystery of sin in the believer's life—that moral dualism that polarizes and paralyzes Christian living and explains why you haven't made progress in your spiritual pilgrimage. That dualism explains why you're so miserable, why worldliness is written across your face, why wastefulness is written across your life, why willfulness is written across your soul. But victory can be yours as you recognize the will of God and surrender to it. When that happens, the Holy Spirit will clothe you with power to see that will of God fulfilled in your life with profit, with pleasure, and with purpose. Hallelujah! But the *issue* is the will of God.

Adelaide Pollard wrote the hymn "Have Thine Own Way, Lord" in 1902 during a time when she was suffering "great distress of soul." Shortly before, she had tried unsuccessfully to raise funds for a missionary trip to Africa. A prayer meeting had brought peace to her heart and complete abandonment of self in submission to God's will. The first verse of that hymn goes like this:

The Signpost of Sinfulness

Have Thine own way, Lord!
Have Thine own way!
Thou art the Potter;
I am the clay.
Mould me and make me
After Thy will,
While I am waiting,
Yielded and still.

FOR FURTHER STUDY

1. Why do believers still struggle with sin after conversion? (See Gal. 5:17.) Where are you struggling currently?

2. Explain the difference between an act of sin and the habit of sin. How do you break a sinful habit? How do you develop a righteous habit? What is God's part in this process? (See 1 John 1:9; Ps. 51:10-11.) What is your part? (See Gal. 5:16; Rom. 6:11-13.)

3. What are some practices that have helped you "walk in the Spirit"? What hinders you? What will you do to overcome the obstacles?

4. What does acceptance of God's will have to do with overcoming the problem of sin? Have you yielded to God's will in *every* area of your life? Why or why not? What verse of Scripture states God's will for your life?

5. To whom does God give His Holy Spirit? (See Acts 5:32.) How does the Holy Spirit help you overcome sin? (See Rom. 8:13.)

The Signpost of
FORGIVENESS

This is the message which we have heard from Him and declare to you, that God is light and in Him is no darkness at all. If we say that we have fellowship with Him, and walk in darkness, we lie and do not practice the truth. But if we walk in the light as He is in the light, we have fellowship with one another, and the blood of Jesus Christ His Son cleanses us from all sin. If we say that we have no sin, we deceive ourselves, and the truth is not in us. If we confess our sins, He is faithful and just to forgive us our sins and to cleanse us from all unrighteousness. If we say that we have not sinned, we make Him a liar, and His word is not in us.

My little children, these things I write to you, so that you may not sin. And if anyone sins, we have an Advocate with the Father, Jesus Christ the righteous. And He Himself is the propitiation for our sins, and not for ours only but also for the whole world.

1 JOHN 1:5–2:2

2

If it is possible for Christians to sin, what hope have we of forgiveness? The answer to that question is dealt with in no uncertain terms in the first chapter of John's first epistle. We must understand, of course, that there can be no forgiveness without the revealing light of God and the cleansing blood of Christ. In the final analysis, transparency of life is fellowship with God and with other Christians who are walking in the light.

The dominant theme of this epistle is fellowship in the life, light, and love of Jesus. Few chapters in the entire Bible reveal more clearly the secret of forgiveness for the Christian. There are three aspects of this forgiveness: first of all, the purpose; secondly, the promise; and thirdly, and most importantly, the power of divine recovery from backsliding and sin. We shall deal with each of these aspects.

THE PURPOSE OF DIVINE FORGIVENESS

"If we say that we have fellowship with Him, and walk in darkness, we lie and do not practice the truth. But if we walk in the light as He is in the light, we have fellowship with one another, and the blood of Jesus Christ His Son cleanses us from all sin" (1 John 1:6-7). The purpose of divine forgiveness is introduced with the statement: "God is light" (1:5). Light condemns sin. Jesus declared, "This is the condemnation, that the light has come into the world, and men loved darkness rather than light, because their deeds were evil. For everyone practicing evil hates the light and does not come to the light, lest his deeds be exposed" (John 3:19-20). On the other hand, light commends truth. Jesus also said, "He who does the truth comes to the light, that his deeds may be clearly seen, that they have been done in God" (John 3:21).

Prevalent in John's day was the heresy of the antinomianists who denied the *peril* of sin in their lives. They believed that the more they sinned, the more God forgave (see Rom. 6:1-2). Therefore, since God's grace was limitless, why should they not go on sinning that grace might abound? Hence, the crisis of the Christian's forgiveness.

The whole purpose of forgiveness is to restore broken fellowship. There is only one thing that breaks fellowship, and that is sin. I believe every Christian should be as sensitive to sin as the eye is to a foreign body. To maintain a life of unbroken fellowship, the Word of God lays down three conditions:

Obedience to the Light of Christ

"If we walk in the light" (1:7). Though scholars differ on the interpretation here, all are agreed that light is God's self-revelation. In the final analysis, when we talk about obedience to the light of Christ, we are talking about following the Lord Jesus who said, "I am the light of the world. He who follows Me shall not walk in darkness, but have the light of life" (John 8:12). Are you walking in the light? Is your obedience up to date? Have you obeyed every word that has come to you through the pulpit or in your own quiet time?

Signposts to Guide Us

The longest known revival in history took place in Rwanda and Uganda, Africa. When a Christian met another Christian and sensed his inner glow waning, the first question asked was, "Are you walking in the light, my brother?"

But not only is there this obedience to the light of Christ, there must be:

Continuance in the Love of Christ

"Fellowship with one another" (1:7). The reference here in verse 7 is to vertical and horizontal fellowship. If we are walking in the light with God, we have fellowship with our brethren. The greatest need in the church of Jesus Christ is an immersion into a new *koinonia*. The reason we don't see revival today is that we are so divided; we do not love one another. The heathen cannot say of us, as they did of the early church, "See how these Christians love one another."

Let me ask you: Are you in fellowship with your husband? Are you in fellowship with your wife? Do you have fellowship with your children, and do your children have fellowship with you? Are you a member of a Christ-exalting, Bible-preaching church? And if so, are you in fellowship with everyone in your church?

But the life of forgiveness also involves:

Experience of the Life of Christ

"The blood of Jesus Christ His Son cleanses us from all sin" (1:7). Theologically, this includes the twin truths of justification and sanctification. That phrase "the blood of Jesus Christ" speaks of the vicarious and victorious death of Christ. When our Lord Jesus Christ died on Calvary's cross and released His life

The Signpost of Forgiveness

through His blood-shedding, He dealt with our sins to justify and also to sanctify us. The only way we can live a pure life is by trusting the indwelling life of Christ. He died and rose to keep us clean. Yes, the blood of Jesus Christ goes on cleansing from every sin on the basis of obedience to the light of Christ, continuance in the love of Christ, and experience in the life of Christ.

There is another heresy that John repudiates. The antinomianists not only denied the peril of sin in the life, but they also denied the *presence* of sin in the life. They contended that the body was just an envelope that enclosed the spirit, so that the spirit could not be touched or defiled by sin. Therefore, they reasoned, the body had nothing to do with the spirit. Such thinking has invaded every society throughout human history. Psychiatrists and psychologists today are telling us that there is no such thing as sin. We behave badly because of our environment. It's just the way we were born.

Have you denied the presence of sin in your life? Do not delude yourself, for until you get to heaven, you are going to have that root of sin in your life. Thank God, there is:

THE PROMISE OF DIVINE FORGIVENESS

"If we confess our sins, He is faithful and just to forgive us our sins and to cleanse us from all unrighteousness" (1:9). The glorious language of this ninth verse undergirds the promise of divine recovery and fellowship with God.

There Is a Sure Foundation for Forgiveness

"If we confess our sins, He is faithful and just to forgive us our sins and to cleanse us from all unrighteousness" (1:9). There are two truths in this foundation: first of all, the *faithfulness of God's Word*—"He is faithful" (1:9). If God says He can forgive you, He will forgive you. He cannot lie.

But more than that, there is *the work of God's righteousness*— "He is . . . just" (1:9). Paul tells us that He is "just and the justifier of the one who has faith in Jesus" (Rom. 3:26). When the Savior hung on Calvary's cross, He cried, "My God, My God, why have You forsaken Me?" (Matt. 27:46). Why was He forsaken? Because He faced the greatest paradox of the ages: "He who knew no sin was made sin; that we might be made the righteousness of God in him" (2 Cor. 5:21).

So we can rest on the promise of divine forgiveness. But more than that:

There Is a Sure Provision for Forgiveness

"He is faithful and just to forgive us our sins and to cleanse us from all unrighteousness" (1:9). In that statement John tells us that *God remits the guilt of sin.* "He is faithful and just to forgive us our sins" (1:9). Taken from an Old Testament ritual, that word *forgive* means to send away. You will remember that on the Day of Atonement, after the high priest had confessed the sins of the people over the head of a live goat, he sent that animal away by the hand of a suitable man into the wilderness (Lev. 16:21). This is a vivid picture of the way God puts away our sins.

☐ *He Sends Our Sins to the Place of No Remembrance.* Isaiah 38:17 tells us that He has cast all our sins behind His back. And Jeremiah 31:34 reminds us that He will forgive our iniquity, and our sin He will remember no more.

☐ *He Sends Our Sins to the Place of No Recovery.* The prophet Micah tells us that He "will cast all our sins into the depths of the sea" (Micah 7:19). Two or three miles off the south coast of England there is a place so deep that all the dissolved sewage of London is released there. Each day of the week, except Sunday, a ship loaded with garbage goes to that spot, and at the press of a button all the filth of the city is pumped into the depths of the sea. The remarkable thing is that minutes later you can fill a glass with that seawater and drink from it without contamination or harm. The sea is so deep that the poison cannot surface. Similarly, God puts our sins into the place of no recovery.

☐ *He Sends Our Sins to the Place of No Return.* "As far as the east is from the west, so far has He removed our transgressions from us" (Ps. 103:12). The point of this great promise is that East and West can *never* meet! The farther east you go, the more distant you are from the west, and vice versa.

But God not only remits the guilt of sin, *He removes the grip of sin.* "He is faithful . . . to cleanse us from all unrighteousness" (1:9). If sin has anything to do with our lives as believers, we become not only defiled, but also defeated. Sin has its stains, and it also has its chains. Thank God, He replaces unrighteousness with the righteousness of our risen Savior. "He breaks the power of cancelled sin."

There Is a Sure Condition for Forgiveness

"If we confess our sins" (1:9). The word *confess* means to agree with God about our sins. This involves deep, radical repentance—a message the Christian church needs today. While it is true that the world is to repent, obey, and believe the Gospel, the Christian needs to repent as well. For "the time has come for judgment to begin at the house of God" (1 Peter 4:17). To confess our sins involves three things:

Signposts to Guide Us

☐ WE MUST TELL GOD ABOUT OUR SINS

We must confess our sins, and this involves:

☐ *Private Confession.* This has to do with God and you. Anything that breaks fellowship must be specifically confessed. Proverbs 28:13 says, "He who covers his sins will not prosper, but whoever confesses and forsakes them will have mercy."

☐ *Personal Confession.* This involves another brother or sister in Christ. Jesus said, "Therefore if you bring your gift to the altar, and there remember that your brother has something against you, leave your gift there before the altar, and go your way. First be reconciled to your brother, and then come and offer your gift" (Matt. 5:23-24). And James adds, "Confess your trespasses to one another, and pray for one another, that you may be healed" (James 5:16).

☐ *Public Confession.* When the sin committed involves the whole church, confession must be made to the whole church before restoration can take place (see Matt. 18:15-17).

☐ WE MUST TRUST GOD ABOUT OUR SINS

"He is faithful . . . to forgive us our sins" (1:9). If He is the God of faithfulness, we can trust Him completely, not only to honor His Word, but also to hear our prayer. He is also the God of righteousness, so He must honor the work of His Son fulfilled for us on Calvary's cross.

☐ WE MUST THANK GOD ABOUT OUR SINS

"He is faithful and just" (1:9). Because He is just, He deals not only with the guilt, but also with the grip of sin, and we must accept His work in us by faith, with thanksgiving. What peace and joy this brings to a believing heart! God has made it so simple: Tell Him, trust Him, and then thank Him. All our requests in prayer are to be made "with thanksgiving" (Phil. 4:6).

But now we come to the most blatant claim of the antinomianists. It is that of denying the *practice* of sin in the life. John's reply to this is both searching and simple: "If we say that we have not sinned, we make [God] a liar, and His word is not in us. My little children, these things I write to you, so that you may not sin. And if anyone sins, we have an Advocate with the Father, Jesus Christ the righteous. And He Himself is the propitiation for our sins, and not for ours only but also for the whole world" (1:10–2:2).

We find similar words in the prophecy of Isaiah: "Woe to those who call evil good, and good evil; who put darkness for light, and light for darkness; who put bitter for sweet, and sweet for bitter! Woe to those who are wise in their own eyes, and prudent in their own sight! Woe to men mighty at drinking wine, woe to men valiant for mixing intoxicating drink, who justify the wicked for a bribe, and take away justice from the righteous man!" (Isa. 5:20-23). How can the believer know recovery in a situation like that? John gives us the answer in:

THE POWER OF DIVINE FORGIVENESS

"My little children, these things I write to you, so that you may not sin" (2:1). God says that even though we sin at times, He has made a way for cleansing and recovery whereby it is possible for us to live victoriously.

When a ship goes out to sea, there are lifeboats on hand, not in order that the ship might sink, but in case the ship does sink! God's provision for forgiveness is no excuse to sin; it is rather to keep us from sinning. "But suppose I do sin?" you ask. "Suppose the power, presence, and practice of sin overcome me?"

John replies, "We have an Advocate with the Father, Jesus Christ the righteous. And He Himself is the propitiation for our sins, and not for ours only but also for the whole world" (2:1-2). Forgiveness is all wrapped up in our blessed Savior, Jesus Christ, the Son of God.

There are three wonderful aspects of this power of God's forgiving grace:

The Power of His Divine Justice

That power is in "Jesus Christ the righteous" (2:1). He alone can determine what is sinful and pronounce the judgment. It is a consolation to know that we have an answer for "the accuser of the brethren" (Rev. 12:10). Whatever the devil might do to try and defeat us, Jesus has the last word. He is always accurate in His judgment.

The Power of His Divine Mercy

"We have an Advocate with the Father, Jesus Christ the righteous" (2:1). An advocate is "one called alongside" to plead our cause. Jesus defends us before the Father's face against all the accusations of self and Satan. What He expects of us, however, is repentance and confession of our sins.

The Power of His Divine Pardon

"He Himself is the propitiation for our sins, and not for ours only but also for the whole world" (2:2). On one occasion the Son of God looked at a paralyzed man brought into His presence for healing. Before He made him stand on his feet in physical wholeness, He said, "Son, your sins are forgiven you" (Mark 2:5). When the religious critics challenged those words of divine pardon, Jesus replied, "The Son of Man has power [or authority] on earth to forgive sins" (Mark 2:10).

You may feel utterly paralyzed because of sin in your life. There stands One alongside you whose accuracy of judgment, advocacy of mercy, and efficacy of pardon are available to you. Therefore, by faith perceive the purpose of forgiveness, by faith believe the promise of forgiveness, and by faith receive the power of forgiveness in Jesus Christ our Lord. Only through the cleansing grace of God can we live transparent lives. We have to face this issue in order to conquer! We are called to a life of victory day by day!

> *There is recovery from my sin,*
> *Thru' Christ who died for me,*
> *Because the vict'ry I can win,*
> *He won—to set me free!*
> S. F. O.

FOR FURTHER STUDY

1. How can you keep your relationship with God from breaking down? (See 1 John 1:7.) What does "walk in the light" mean?

2. Are any of your relationships with people broken? Do you need to forgive someone? Do you need to ask someone for forgiveness? Ask God to help you repair the break.

3. What is the only way to keep your life pure? (See Rom. 6:4-7.) Explain the believer's union with Christ. How are we one with Him?

4. Are there any sinful behaviors in your life that have been there so long they just seem normal? Mark any of the following

excuses you've been making. Put a star by the ones you think God will accept.

"I've always been this way."

"A temper runs in the family."

"This is just a *little* sin."

"Everybody does it."

"It doesn't hurt anyone else."

"I'm only human."

"I tried to stop and failed."

Remember: *any* sin not only defiles but defeats us. "Sin not only has its stains but its chains." Do not excuse sin any longer.

5. What characterizes true confession? How many times will God forgive you?

The Signpost of
HOLINESS

✳

*Therefore gird up the loins of your mind, be sober, and rest
your hope fully upon the grace that is to be brought to you
at the revelation of Jesus Christ; as obedient children, not
conforming yourselves to the former lusts, as in your igno-
rance; but as He who called you is holy, you also be holy in
all your conduct, because it is written, "Be holy, for I am
holy." And if you call on the Father, who without partiality
judges according to each one's work, conduct yourselves
throughout the time of your stay here in fear; knowing that
you were not redeemed with corruptible things, like silver or
gold, from your aimless conduct received by tradition from
your fathers, but with the precious blood of Christ, as of a
lamb without blemish and without spot. He indeed was fore-
ordained before the foundation of the world, but was manifest in these last times for you who through Him believe in
God, who raised Him from the dead and gave Him glory, so
that your faith and hope are in God. Since you have purified
your souls in obeying the truth through the Spirit in sincere
love of the brethren, love one another fervently with a pure
heart, having been born again, not of corruptible seed but
incorruptible, through the word of God which lives and
abides forever, because*

The Signpost of Holiness

"All flesh is as grass,
And all the glory of man
*   as the flower of the grass.*
The grass withers,
And its flower falls away,
But the word of the LORD
*   endures forever."*

Now this is the word which by the gospel was preached to you.

1 PETER 1:13-25

3

Holiness is a subject that frightens most people. In one sense, this can be readily understood, especially when we read a verse such as, "Be holy, for I am holy" (v. 16) and then thoughtfully consider what the holiness of God means.

The Scriptures teach us that God is holy in His being: "You are holy, enthroned in the praises of Israel" (Ps. 22:3). We cannot reflect upon the nature of His being without reverently exclaiming, "Holy, holy, holy is the Lord of hosts; the whole earth is full of His glory!" (Isa. 6:3).

Then the Bible makes it clear that He is holy in His speaking: "God has spoken in His holiness" (Ps. 60:6). We can read the literary giants of all time and be inspired and edified, but when we take up the Word of God and hear God speaking in holiness, we are searched and sanctified to the very depths of our personalities.

Once again the sacred record reveals that God is holy in His working: "The Lord is righteous in all His ways, gracious in all His works" (Ps. 145:17). The activity of God is always characterized by justice, righteousness, and holiness.

Thus we see that the entire subject of holiness is awesome, and yet on the other hand, holiness is the key to a life of healthiness and happiness. That is why Jesus said, "Blessed are the pure in heart, for they shall see God" (Matt. 5:8). It behooves us, therefore, to understand scriptural holiness if we would know lives that are spiritually healthy and happy. Let us start with:

THE DEFINITION OF HOLINESS

"Be holy, for I am holy" (v. 16). These words constitute a divine command, and failure to obey them is serious sin. In order to understand what is meant by scriptural holiness, we must define the word *holy* or *holiness*. There is:

The Old Testament Word

In the Old Testament, the term *holy*, with all its cognates, is invariably derived from a Hebrew word that suggests sanctity or a setting apart of the thing described as sacred to the purposes of God alone. The vessels of the ancient sanctuary were said to be holy or set apart for God's use, and so the exhortation addressed to those who served in the tabernacle was, "Be clean, you who bear the vessels of the LORD" (Isa. 52:11).

Then there is:

The New Testament Word

The New Testament employs another word for holiness and sanctification. Although the etymology is not the same as that used in the Old Testament, the meaning of the word is basically the same. The New Testament word signifies something full of awe or awe-inspiring, because the thing or person so described belongs peculiarly and only to God.

In New York City, where I served as pastor of Calvary Baptist Church for fourteen years, are two well-known buildings—the Waldorf Astoria and Gracie Mansion. Both are imposing as to their accommodations and appointments. But there is a distinct difference between them when it comes to their use. You and I can enter the Waldorf Astoria Hotel at any time and enjoy a meal or a night's lodging, provided we meet the financial conditions. But Gracie Mansion is reserved for one purpose alone, and that is to house the mayor, his family, and distinguished guests that he may invite. This setting apart of Gracie Mansion for the mayor's use alone illustrates the meaning of the New Testament word that is translated holy. When God saves men and women, He not only imparts holiness, as we shall see in a moment, but constitutes them holy and sets them apart for His purpose alone.

But once again there is:

The Anglo-Saxon Word

The term *holiness* comes from the Anglo-Saxon root *halig*, which means soundness and completeness. From this derivation has come into present-day use our words *healthiness* and *wholeness*.

The essence of holiness, then, is the sum of this threefold definition. We might state it as follows. Given spiritual life, holiness means the maintaining in health of that life before God and the setting apart of that life for His service alone.

In the next place, I want you to consider:

THE IMPARTATION OF HOLINESS

"Be holy, for I am holy" (v. 16). This mandate from heaven was never designed to tantalize or torment us. God never makes a demand without providing the dynamic. So we learn from the Scriptures and, in terms of spiritual experience, that:

The Signpost of Holiness

Holiness Is Provided by God

"Christ ... became for us ... sanctification [or holiness]" (1 Cor. 1:30). This simply means that God makes this holiness available to us by the incoming and indwelling life of the Lord Jesus. The holiness that the Savior preached, practiced, and purchased is imparted to "the vilest offender who truly believes." Herein is the glory of the Gospel of Christ. Peter, in his epistle, tells us that through the effectual calling of God we are made "partakers of the divine nature" (2 Peter 1:4); and the writer to the Hebrews informs us that we are "partakers of His holiness" (Heb. 12:10).

So we see that in no way whatsoever is holiness the product of human effort. It is rather a work of God made effective in us by the indwelling life of Christ, through the power of the Holy Spirit.

Holiness Is Preserved by God

Addressing the Thessalonians, Paul prays, "May the God of peace Himself sanctify you completely; and may your whole spirit, soul, and body be preserved blameless at the coming of our Lord Jesus Christ. He who calls you is faithful, who also will do it" (1 Thess. 5:23-24). The term *holiness*, as we have seen already, means wholeness or healthiness, and this, as we gather from Paul's words, implies the preservation of a healthy spirit, soul, and body. So God, who is faithful, undertakes to keep us holy. To understand how God works to preserve us "blameless at the coming of our Lord Jesus Christ," we need to observe the divine action delineated in this remarkable verse.

☐ GOD DECLARES HIS PURPOSE TO MAKE US HOLY

"May your whole spirit, soul, and body be preserved blameless" (1 Thess. 5:23). In Paul's prayer, God's purpose is clear.

Signposts to Guide Us

Every area of our lives must be holy. The spirit must be conse-
crated, the soul must be separated, and the body must be dedicated to God's holy purpose. Without holiness "no one will see
the Lord" (Heb. 12:14).

☐ GOD DESIGNS HIS PROCESS TO MAKE US HOLY

"He who calls you is faithful, who also will do it" (1 Thess.
5:24). This process is focused on His continuing effectual call to
those who have been chosen in Christ before the foundation of
the world. The continuing call is effected daily by the Word of
God; hence the need for our consistent quiet time with the Lord.
Jesus prayed, "Sanctify them by Your truth. Your word is truth"
(John 17:17).

Dr. Harry A. Ironside tells how he answered people who
claimed to be "completely sanctified." He would ask them if
they had read through *all* the Bible. Invariably, they would reply
in the negative. His retort was always the same: "How can you
be completely sanctified if you have never read your Bible
completely?"

☐ GOD DIRECTS HIS POWER TO MAKE US HOLY

"He who calls you is faithful, who also will do it [or perform
it]" (1 Thess. 5:24). The little word *it* is not in the original text. The
verse there reads, "Faithful is he who goes on calling, who also
will do." The *absolute* use of the verb *do* is very striking. God is
both the Caller and the Doer. He exercises His power to perform
and complete in us His holy will. It is the power of His Holy
Spirit, working to do in us His perfect will—hence our need not
only to be *fed* on the Word but to be *filled* with the Spirit. The command is clear: Go on being "filled with the Spirit" (Eph. 5:18). It

is a *command*, and failure to obey it is sin. If we would be holy, we must be controlled by the Holy Spirit.

So we must glorify God in our spirits, in our souls, and in our bodies. What a comfort to know that God has promised to preserve us "blameless at the coming of our Lord Jesus Christ" (1 Thess. 5:23). The evidence that He is being allowed to do this in our lives is that there is harmony, happiness, and healthiness existing in these three realms of our personalities. This is why He prays that "the God of peace [should] sanctify [us] completely . . . spirit, soul, and body" (1 Thess. 5:23).

Once again:

Holiness Is Perfected by God

John tells us that "when He is revealed, we shall be like Him, for we shall see Him as He is" (1 John 3:2). The final realization of this perfection of holiness will be experienced at the coming again of our Lord and Savior Jesus Christ. The sense in which we are perfected is that in that day our redeemed spirits, souls, and bodies will be identified completely with the life of Christ that was imparted to us when we first believed. Thus we see there is going to be a perfection of consummation when we get to heaven. In the meantime, however, the Word of God insists that there should be a perfection of condition in our present-day experience of holiness.

This brings us to the third aspect of our subject:

THE ATTESTATION OF HOLINESS

"But as He who called you is holy, you also be holy in all your conduct" (1 Peter 1:15). It is quite clear from that statement that holiness makes certain demands upon us. There cannot be an impartation of holiness without an attestation of holiness. This is what Paul means when he says, "God did not call us to uncleanness, but in holiness" (1 Thess. 4:7).[1] From other passages of the Word of God, it appears that the attestation of scriptural holiness is twofold:

Yieldedness to God

"Present your members as slaves of righteousness for holiness" (Rom. 6:19), or more literally, "present your members as servants of righteousness commensurate with a life of holiness." A believer who is living a life of practical holiness will know what it is to be completely and continually yielded to God. Such yieldedness implies a once-for-all act of surrender followed by a daily attitude of surrender. This implies a life of development and of discipline.

When the apostle appeals to the believers at Rome to yield their bodies to God as a "reasonable service," he specifies that the sacrifice is to be "living . . . holy, [and] acceptable" (Rom. 12:1). So many Christians imagine that they can dedicate to God lives that are defiled and defeated, but the teaching of this verse makes it quite clear that such a sacrifice is unacceptable (see Mal. 3:8-10). We are to yield or present our members as servants of righteousness commensurate with a life of holiness.

The second attestation of holiness is:

Fruitfulness for God

"But now having been set free from sin, and having become slaves of God, you have your fruit to holiness" (Rom. 6:22). Fruitfulness follows yieldedness. This is a divine order that cannot be reversed. Indeed, it is because we so often try to reverse this law of spiritual life that our acts of dedication and surrender never last. Obedience to God must precede our offering to God. This fruit of holiness includes:

☐ FRUITFULNESS IN OUR CHRISTIAN WORSHIP

Writing to the Hebrews, the apostle says, "Let us continually offer the sacrifice of praise to God, that is, the fruit of our lips, giving thanks to His name" (Heb. 13:15). God longs for our worship. Jesus revealed that "the Father is seeking such [as we are] to worship Him" (John 4:23). Day by day, and particularly Sunday by Sunday, He waits for our baskets of firstfruits. Indeed, the phrase "fruit to holiness" (Rom. 6:22) is a reference to the Old Testament idea of bringing the firstfruits of the land as an act of worship to God (see Ex. 23:16; Prov. 3:9). That which was required physically then is what God desires spiritually now. We must see to it, however, that our sacrifice of praise is the fruit of obedience and holiness.

☐ FRUITFULNESS IN OUR CHRISTIAN WALK

"By this My Father is glorified, that you bear much fruit; so you will be My disciples" (John 15:8). Such fruitfulness in Christian character glorifies God because it is the exhibition of the very life of Christ. Paul speaks of it as "the fruit of the Spirit [which] is love, joy, peace, longsuffering, kindness, goodness, faithfulness, gentleness, self-control" (Gal. 5:22-23). There is no greater argument for the reality of Christian experience than a Christlike character.

A lovely story from England is told of the saintly Thomas Cook, who was due to visit a certain home. The husband and wife were determined to give him a royal welcome and make sure that all his temporal needs were cared for. The unconverted maid rebelled against all the work of preparation, so when she visited the butcher for the weekend roast, she vented her feelings: "I don't know who this Mr. Cook is, but you would think that he was the Almighty Himself, judging by the fuss that is being made." A week later the maid returned to the butcher shop very subdued and quiet. The man at the counter, observing this, asked her how she was getting on with the visitor. Softly she whispered, "I am sorry for what I said last week. The Reverend Thomas Cook is the most wonderful man I've ever met. When he's around, it makes you feel as if God is in the house."

□ FRUITFULNESS IN OUR CHRISTIAN WORK

Addressing His disciples, Jesus said, "You did not choose Me, but I chose you and appointed you that you should go and bear *fruit*, and that your *fruit* should remain" (John 15:16). Writing to the Romans, Paul expressed his longing that he might have some *fruit* among them also, "just as among the other Gentiles" (Rom. 1:13).

Is your life one of fruitfulness in service? Are you reproducing the life of Christ in others by the way you live and preach the Gospel? Is there evidence around you that you have been chosen and ordained to bring forth lasting fruit? If your answer is in the negative, then you know nothing of practical holiness in your life. What the world needs to see is a Christian church made up of men and women who manifest in their daily living a quality of life that characterized our Lord Jesus Christ. All manner of extreme teaching has been associated with the word *holiness*, but this is not scriptural holiness! Holiness, in terms of biblical truth, is both redemptive and productive. It not only changes the life, but challenges us to live and preach Jesus Christ.

So we have seen what we mean by the definition, impartation, and attestation of holiness. May we be determined to be holy, even as God is holy, for without such holiness "no one will see the Lord" (Heb. 12:14). Let our daily prayer be:

> *Jesus, my Savior, in my behavior,*
> *Help me to be like Thee;*
> *Harmless and holy, loving and lowly*
> *Patient and pure like Thee!*
> E. H. G. SARGENT

FOR FURTHER STUDY

1. Define holiness. What are your first thoughts or impressions when you hear that word?

2. In asking us to be holy, has God given us an impossible command? Why or why not?

3. Explain the difference between the position and the process of a believer's holiness. (See 1 Cor. 1:30; 2 Peter 1:4.) What part does human effort play in our position before God?

4. How do you become holy in the way you live daily? (See John 17:17; Rom. 6:19.) How do you get the Word of God into your heart as well as into your head? Give examples of how you would put Romans 6:19 into practice. How much are you depending on the indwelling Holy Spirit to be your righteousness in the difficulties and temptations you are now facing?

5. What is necessary for a believer to produce the fruit of holiness? Name some of the fruit. What glorious reward is offered to those who are pure? (See Matt. 5:8.)

The Signpost of

CHRIST-CENTEREDNESS

I have been crucified with Christ; it is no longer I who live, but Christ lives in me; and the life which I now live in the flesh I live by faith in the Son of God, who loved me and gave Himself for me. I do not set aside the grace of God; for if righteousness comes through the law, then Christ died in vain. O foolish Galatians! Who has bewitched you that you should not obey the truth, before whose eyes Jesus Christ was clearly portrayed among you as crucified? This only I want to learn from you: Did you receive the Spirit by the works of the law, or by the hearing of faith? Are you so foolish? Having begun in the Spirit, are you now being made perfect by the flesh? Have you suffered so many things in vain—if indeed it was in vain? Therefore He who supplies the Spirit to you and works miracles among you, does He do it by the works of the law, or by the hearing of faith?—just as Abraham "believed God, and it was accounted to him for righteousness." Therefore know that only those who are of faith are sons of Abraham.

GALATIANS 2:20–3:7

The Signpost of
CHRIST-CENTEREDNESS

4

The greatest moment in my life was when I discovered that God expects nothing more or less of Stephen Olford than abject failure! And, even more importantly, only one Person can live the Christian life, and that is Christ Himself; and only as I trust Him to live His life in me, can I possibly live the quality of life that satisfies the heart of God and challenges the world in which I witness.

So many people imagine that the Christian life is *their* attempt to live as Christians. It can't be done. We can't keep the Ten Commandments; we can't keep the Sermon on the Mount; we can't keep the absolutes of the Word of God.

There is only one Person who ever did it, and that was the Lord Jesus Christ Himself, who contracted to the measure of a woman's womb, was born as a babe, and lived among men. After thirty years of solitude and silence (except for one flower that was thrown over the wall of His boyhood days), nobody knew anything about Him. That was His hidden life.

But when He stood on the banks of the Jordan, God broke through from heaven and declared, "This is My beloved Son, in whom I am well pleased" (Matt. 3:17). Having pleased His father in His hidden life, He launched upon His ministry. On the

---

Mount of Transfiguration, He stood there as One who had been tested by friends, foes, and fiends. At that point in time, God broke through from heaven again and said, "This is My beloved Son, in whom I am well pleased. Hear Him!" (Matt. 17:5).

In His private life, He pleased the Father. In His public life, He pleased the Father. And having demonstrated how the Christian life was to be lived, He went to Calvary and shed His blood on the cross to clean up the mess that you and I had made. Then He went to heaven in His resurrection power to pour out the Holy Spirit to indwell you and me. That is our Gospel!

Although born on a mission station in the heart of Africa, and sitting under the ministry of my godly father, I have to confess that it wasn't until the age of twenty-one that I came to understand this message. Jesus said, "Without Me you can do nothing" (John 15:5). Thank God that all the carnal strivings are over in my attempt to live the Christian life. Now I say, "I can't, but, Lord Jesus, You can! 'Jesus, be Jesus in me. No longer me, but Thee. Resurrection power, fill me this hour. Jesus, be Jesus in me.'"

So my message is Christ-centeredness. Two aspects of this truth are taught in our text.

THE TERMINATION OF THE SELF-LIFE

"I have been crucified with Christ" (2:20). The verb is in the past tense, but what happened in *history* now happens in *victory* in my life! That is why the King James Version reads, "I am crucified with Christ." The fact is that when Jesus died at Calvary's cross, He not only died for me, but I died with Him, for God doesn't crucify what He has not condemned. So there must be:

Signposts to Guide Us

The Condemnation of the Self-Life

"I have been crucified with Christ" (2:20). This glorious truth changed the life of Martin Luther, John Calvin, all the great reformers, yes, and simple Christians down through the centuries. When Paul says, "I have been crucified with Christ," he is restating what he has affirmed in his Roman epistle: "For what the law could not do in that it was weak through the flesh, God did by sending His own Son in the likeness of sinful flesh, on account of sin: *He condemned sin in the flesh,* that the righteous requirement of the law might be fulfilled in us who do not walk according to the flesh but according to the Spirit" (8:3-4).

The self-life is sin in the flesh, and God has condemned it. When the Lord Jesus Christ came, He not only embodied and expounded the Law, but He *exacted* the Law. He exacted it by taking the penalty of your sin and my sin at Calvary and paying our sin debt on the cross. So he condemned sin in the flesh. Anyone who tries to perfect the flesh, which is the humanistic view in our religious world today, is violating the very truth of God. But what God condemns, He crucifies.

The Crucifixion of the Self-Life

"Knowing this, that our old man was crucified with Him, that the body of sin might be done away with, that we should no longer be slaves of sin" (Rom. 6:6). The crucified life is an important doctrine. If we do not accept our crucifixion, how can we accept our resurrection in Christ? One of the great truths that has transformed my life is the fact that "Christ died for our sins according to the Scriptures, and that He was buried, and that He rose again the third day according to the Scriptures" (1 Cor. 15:3-4).

Soon after I understood this message, I went out to preach,

but the Devil kept saying to me, "Stephen, how can you dare to preach the victorious life? Just think back a few years to your backsliding days and the dreadful life you lived then." The Devil paralyzed me; he shut my mouth; he silenced my witness.

But in my distress I went to hear a missionary who was expounding the early chapters of the Roman epistle. He came to chapter 6 and said, "I wonder if there is a young man here this evening who once had a glowing testimony, but now you are totally paralyzed. You are obsessed with introspection, and the Devil is saying to you, 'You know what you were. What a hypocrite you are to open your mouth now.'" Then this dear man of God, in the flow of his message, pointed his finger at the audience and said, "Beloved young man, if you are sitting here tonight, I want to tell you that you are violating the law of Romans 6. You were buried! What God condemns, He crucifies. What God crucifies, He buries. What is buried, *you are not to dig up.*"

As I heard those words, God set me free! I saw the truth that Christ died for me; I died with Him. He went into the grave, and so did I. On the basis of that death and burial, I can claim resurrection life! If you want to know Christ's resurrection power released in you, then sincerely pray, "Lord, I am dead, but alive in You. 'Resurrection power, fill me this hour. Jesus, be Jesus in me.'" This is the termination of the self-life.

Romans 8:13 gives an exposition of this doctrine of the crucified life. "For if you live according to the flesh," that is, the self-life, "you will die." Everything you touch will die. Your preaching will die, your praying will die, your quiet time will die, and your witnessing will die. "But if by the Spirit you put to death [go on putting to death—present tense] the deeds of the body, you will live."

There is a clear distinction between biblical crucifixion and self-mutilation. You do not have to go to a monastery in order to mutilate yourself! That is not what the Bible says. You cannot crucify yourself; it is one death that *you cannot self-inflict.* You have to *be crucified.* That is exactly how the Lord Jesus died. But before bowing His head and dying with power, He cried victoriously, "It is finished!" (John 19:30). "He was crucified in weakness" (2 Cor. 13:4). Contradiction? No. Paul is explaining that when He came to Golgotha, He did not struggle. Instead, He gave His hands to be crucified, He gave His feet to be crucified, He gave Himself to be crucified. How did He do that? He "through the eternal Spirit offered Himself without spot" to be crucified (Heb. 9:14).

How am I to be crucified? By the same Spirit. So as I live my life moment by moment and sense self rearing its ugly head, I count on the Holy Spirit to put to death the deeds of the body (Rom. 8:12). Crucifixion is not an *instantaneous* death. It's a lingering death 'til Jesus comes. "A thousand times" a day I have to say, "Lord Jesus, I sense self rising." I have a "little radar" that the Lord has put in my life! The radar catches the vibes from self. It may be that I have said an unkind word to my wife. It may be that I have rebuked my children without the spirit of love. It may be that I have taken glory to myself when someone praises me. I say, "Holy Spirit, nail it." And that is precisely what He does. Self goes to the cross where self belongs, and Jesus comes through my personality in all the glory of His presence and power. This is the termination of the self-life.

What a relief to sing:

STEPHEN F. OLFORD

The Signpost of Christ-Centeredness

> *Oh, to be saved from myself, dear Lord,*
> *Oh, to be lost in Thee;*
> *Oh, that it may be no more I,*
> *But Christ that lives in me.*
> A. A. WHIDDINGTON

That is why Paul says in the epistle to the Romans, "Reckon yourselves to be dead indeed to sin, but alive to God in Christ Jesus our Lord" (6:11). But now let us move on to the next aspect of our subject.

THE SUBSTITUTION OF THE CHRIST-LIFE

"I have been crucified with Christ; it is no longer I who live, but Christ lives in me; and the life which I now live in the flesh I live by faith in the Son of God, who loved me and gave Himself for me" (2:20). I want to say two main things about the substitution of the Christ-life:

We Must Appreciate the Christ-Life

"The life which I now live in the flesh I live by faith in the Son of God, who loved me and gave Himself for me" (2:20). Rightly understood, the Christ-life is:

☐ A DISTINCTIVE LIFE

"Life . . . in the Son of God" (2:20). Peter tells us that we are "partakers of the divine nature" (2 Peter 1:4). The greatest interpreter of the Bible is the Bible. In Romans 1:3-4 Paul says, "Jesus Christ our Lord . . . declared to be the Son of God." The word *declared* actually means "horizoned." Just as we look over a flat horizon as something appears, and it is made to look real by the very backdrop of the horizon, so Jesus Christ was horizoned "to be the Son of God with power, according to the Spirit of holiness, by the resurrection from the dead." This distinctive life that you and I have in us has the *nature of deity*. We are "partakers of the divine nature" (2 Peter 1:4).

Not only do we have the nature of deity, but we also have the *nature of purity*—"the spirit of holiness." By the Spirit, the holy Christ now lives in us. The doctrine of holiness has been lowered and reduced to such meaninglessness in the church today. God wants holy preachers, holy wives, holy laymen, and a holy church. Without holiness "no one will see the Lord" (Heb.12:14). I want this body of mine to be the vehicle for the expression of divine holiness.

The distinctive life is not only the nature of deity and purity, but thirdly, it is the *nature of victory;* for Romans 1:3-4 says, "Jesus Christ our Lord" horizoned "to be the Son of God with power [the nature of deity], according to the Spirit of holiness [the nature of purity], by the resurrection from the dead [the nature of victory]." We need to live the familiar song "Victory in Jesus." I believe it is the purpose of God that we should daily know victory over the world, the self, and the Devil—victory over sin and self and Satan.

Catch Paul's heartthrob, "My beloved brethren, be steadfast, immovable, always abounding in the work of the Lord, knowing that your labor is not in vain in the Lord" (1 Cor. 15:58). Before that he says, "Thanks be to God, who gives us the victory through our Lord Jesus Christ" (1 Cor. 15:57). And, "We are more than conquerors through Him who loved us" (Rom. 8:37). There should never be a pessimistic Christian or a defeatist Christian in the church! We are on the victory side. We may lose a battle here and there, but we do not lose the war. Why? Because He gives us the victory. So this life in Christ is distinctive. It has the nature of deity, purity, and victory. The Christ-life is:

☐ A DEPENDENT LIFE

"I live by faith in the Son of God, who loved me and gave Himself for me (2:20). When we read Hebrews 12:2, we tend to forget that the author writes, "Looking unto Jesus the author and finisher of our faith" (KJV). It is not *our* faith; it is His faith. When Hudson Taylor was striving in missionary work with a sense of defeat, he came upon that verse in Mark: "Have faith in God" (11:22). Using his Greek testament, he translated it to mean "have the faith *of* God." Hold fast the faith (or faithfulness) of God. It is not our faith. Our faith becomes purified in His faith. It is His faith. Remember that in His perfect humanity Jesus lived by faith. This is seen in the areas of:

☐ *His Life.* "As the living Father sent Me, and I live because of the Father, so he who feeds on Me will live because of Me" (John 6:57). The Lord Jesus would not live to the glory of God, save by faith.

☐ *His Work.* "Most assuredly, I say to you, the Son can do nothing of Himself, but what He sees the Father do; for whatever He does, the Son also does in like manner" (John 5:19). The Lord Jesus would not work to the glory of God, save by faith.

☐ *His Words.* "Do you not believe that I am in the Father, and the Father in Me? The words that I speak to you I do not speak on My own authority; but the Father who dwells in Me does the works" (John 14:10). The Lord Jesus would not speak to the glory of God, save by faith. He lived by faith. If in His humanity He chose to live by faith, how do you expect to live? The only answer

Signposts to Guide Us

is: "It is no longer I who live, but Christ lives in me; and the life which I now live in the flesh I live by faith in the Son of God" (2:20).

> *Moment by moment I'm kept in His love,*
> *Moment by moment I've life from above;*
> *Looking to Jesus till glory does shine,*
> *Moment by moment, O Lord, I am Thine.*
> DANIEL W. WHITTLE

The Christ-life is:

□ A DEVOTED LIFE

"It is no longer I who live, but Christ lives in me; and the life which I now live in the flesh I live by faith *in the Son of God, who loved me and gave Himself for me*" (2:20). The literal translation is that He "gave Himself *up* for me." What does that mean? Three important characterizations:

□ *It Is the Life of Submission.* "Behold, I have come—in the volume of the book it is written of Me—to do Your will, O God" (Heb. 10:7; see Ps. 40:7-8), declared the Lord Jesus in the language of the prophecy. When He came to this earth, He reiterated, "My food is to do the will of Him who sent Me, and to finish His work" (John 4:34). When He came to the garden of Gethsemane, He repeated, "Father, if it is possible, let this cup pass from Me; nevertheless, not as I will, but as You will" (Matt. 26:39). This is the life of submission. *He gave Himself up.* What we need are Christians who know the life of submission.

□ *It Is the Life of Sacrifice.* The words "He gave himself up" suggest the death on the cross. "Being in the form of God, [He] did not consider it robbery to be equal with God. . . . He humbled Himself and became obedient to the point of death, even the death of the cross" (Phil. 2:6-8). And "though He was a Son, yet He learned obedience by the things which He suffered" (Heb. 5:8). Submission, and then sacrifice.

☐ *It Is the Life of Service.* "The Son of God . . . gave Himself" (2:20). Earlier in His earthly life Jesus said, "The Son of Man did not come to be served, but to serve, and to give His life" (Matt. 20:28). We are here not only to demonstrate divine submission and divine sacrifice, but also divine service. That means to "love God and love our neighbor"—without discrimination or hesitation.

We must appreciate this Christ-life. What is it? It is a distinctive, dependent, and devoted life. It is the *normal* Christian life. Then secondly:

We Must Appropriate the Christ-Life

"No longer I . . . but Christ" (2:20). So our motto becomes, "Not I, but Christ." Once we have mastered the simple interpretation of the theology of this text, the next thing is to put it to the test. If Christ is all that we have already deduced from our study, then there is no problem. *He is totally adequate.*

One of the greatest preachers of this message was Dr. Alan Redpath. He loved to tell the story of a South African millionaire who bought a Rolls Royce for $70,000. So impressed was he with this car that he wanted to know everything about it, and so he asked the agent about every detail—including the horsepower. The agent gave all the information he could, save the one item of horsepower. He explained, "We are not allowed to divulge this, and in any case, I don't know the answer." But the millionaire insisted on knowing, and so the agent promised to investigate the matter further. He telegraphed London and gave all the specifications of this particular car and then asked them to wire information concerning the horsepower. A brief time elapsed, and then a telegram signed by Rolls Royce came back to the agent. The message was one word: "Adequate!"

As you and I face the problems of everyday life, each one of us can say, "Lord Jesus, You are living in me. You are adequate. My marriage is on the rocks, and I don't know how to handle it, but You have written the blueprint. There must be an answer in You. You are adequate. Lord, I've been hit with financial tragedy, but when all else is taken from me, You are adequate. Temptation is facing me right now, and I sense I may fall, so I appeal to You."

He says to you, "I am adequate." This is the message we desperately need in the church today. The focus across our religious work is "not Christ, but *I*." We have to get the message across to "all and sundry" that it is "not I, but *Christ*."

So we have seen what is meant by the termination of the self-life: God has condemned it; God has crucified it. We must believe that, for it is a basic tenet of our Christian faith. But we must go further, to the substitution of the Christ-life. We must appreciate the fact that the Christ-life is distinctive with the nature of deity, of purity, of victory. It depends by faith on Christ to be and do in us what we cannot achieve by ourselves. It is devoted in terms of submission, sacrifice, and service. We give ourselves up to God and to others in love. "Without Me," said Jesus, "you can do nothing" (John 15:5). But by His indwelling, through the power of the Holy Spirit, He is *adequate*. Only one Person in the whole world lived the Christian life, and that was Jesus. There is only one Person who can live the Christian life now, and that is Jesus. Therefore, exchange all your strivings and defeats in the flesh for His life in you. Make your motto and motivation, "not I, but Christ." This is Christ-centeredness!

> *Jesus, be Jesus in me,*
> *No longer me, but Thee;*
> *Resurrection power, fill me this hour,*
> *Jesus, be Jesus in me.*
> AUTHOR UNKNOWN

FOR FURTHER STUDY

1. Who alone can live the Christian life? How does that truth affect your efforts to live as a Christian? Be practical and specific.

2. In what sense did you die with Christ on the cross? How does this fact affect the way you approach temptations? (See Rom. 6:11.) Several versions of the Bible use the word *reckon*. What does it mean? Compare in other versions.

3. Is the termination of the self-life a process or a one-time event? Explain your answer.

4. What are some characteristics of the new life we have in Christ? (See 2 Peter 1:4; Heb. 12:14; Rom. 8:37.) How do we get these qualities?

5. How do we appropriate the Christ-life? (See Gal. 2:20.) How does this work? If you can, give an example from your own life.

✳

Receive one who is weak in the faith, but not to disputes over doubtful things. For one believes he may eat all things, but he who is weak eats only vegetables. Let not him who eats despise him who does not eat, and let not him who does not eat judge him who eats; for God has received him. Who are you to judge another's servant? To his own master he stands or falls. Indeed, he will be made to stand, for God is able to make him stand. One person esteems one day above another; another esteems every day alike. Let each be fully convinced in his own mind. He who observes the day, observes it to the Lord; and he who does not observe the day, to the Lord he does not observe it. He who eats, eats to the Lord, for he gives God thanks; and he who does not eat, to the Lord he does not eat, and gives God thanks. For none of us lives to himself, and no one dies to himself. For if we live, we live to the Lord; and if we die, we die to the Lord. Therefore, whether we live or die, we are the Lord's. For to this end Christ died and rose and lived again, that He might be Lord of both the dead and the living. But why do you judge your brother? Or why do you show contempt for your brother? For we shall all stand before the judgment seat of Christ. For it is written:

STEPHEN F. OLFORD

The Signpost of Yieldedness

*"As I live, says the LORD,
Every knee shall bow to Me,
And every tongue shall confess to God."*

*So then each of us shall give
account of himself to God.*

ROMANS 14:1-12

5

The central message of the Bible is that "Jesus Christ is Lord." All of history moves to that moment, in God's timing, when every creature will declare that "Jesus Christ is Lord, to the glory of God the Father" (Phil. 2:11).

If we start with that presupposition, then it follows that the crisis of yieldedness in the Christian's life is surrender to the lordship of Christ. To think and work this through, let us turn to the opening verses of Romans 14, where Paul's aim was to silence a dispute threatening the church at Rome. The two vexing questions upon which a difference of opinion had arisen were the keeping of the Sabbath and the eating of certain meats. Without attempting to defend or condemn the opposing groups, Paul taught that the final solution to all matters of faith and conduct was submission to the sovereignty of Jesus Christ. Where Christ was Lord of thinking, speaking, and acting, there would be a corresponding oneness in the life of the church. Thus he reaches a climax where he declares, "For to this end Christ died and rose and lived again, that He might be Lord" (v. 9). To understand this issue of yieldedness, we must note carefully:

The Signpost of Yieldedness

THE RIGHTS OF DIVINE LORDSHIP

"To this end Christ died and rose and lived again, that He might be Lord" (v. 9). The death and resurrection of Jesus Christ are associated inseparably with His lordship. Indeed, we completely misunderstand the purpose of our Savior's redemptive work if we lose sight of the fact that He died and rose in order that "He might be Lord of both the dead and the living" (v. 9). So Paul asserts in unmistakable terms that:

As Lord, Christ Alone Has the Right to Purchase Us

"To this end Christ died . . . that He might be Lord" (v. 9). Already in this epistle Paul has declared that we are "carnal, sold under sin" (7:14); but the wonder of the Gospel is that seeing us in this condition, the Lord Jesus came from heaven's glory to redeem and set us free. In order to do this, however, He had to purchase us and make us His very own, for only in Christ can any man be set free. It is not without significance, therefore, that the idea inherent in the word *Lord* is ownership or proprietorship. So Paul reminds us that we belong to "the church of God which He purchased with His own blood" (Acts 20:28); and again, "You were bought at a price; therefore glorify God in your body and in your spirit, which are God's" (1 Cor. 6:20). Peter also recalls that we "were not redeemed with corruptible things, like silver or gold . . . but with the precious blood of Christ" (1 Peter 1:18-19). It is clear, then, that Jesus died to purchase us completely.

So as we consider ourselves in the totality of our faculties, we are obliged to acknowledge that there is no part of us that has not been bought outright. Christ alone owns our eyes to view His world. He alone owns our hands to serve His will. He alone owns our feet to walk His way. He alone owns our minds to think His thoughts. He alone owns our hearts to love Him fervently. He alone owns our personalities to radiate His charm and glory. Failure to recognize this is a refusal to recognize His sovereignty.

As Lord, Christ Alone Has the Right to Pardon Us

"To this end Christ died and rose" (v. 9). Earlier in this epistle Paul has affirmed that Christ "was delivered up because of our offenses, and was raised because of our justification" (Rom. 4:25). During His life and ministry here on earth, Jesus demonstrated His right to pardon men and women. Recall the occasion when the paralyzed man was borne by four men to the house where Jesus was preaching. They uncovered the roof, lowered the infirm man, and laid him at Jesus' feet. And we read, "When Jesus saw their faith, He said to the paralytic, 'Son, your sins are forgiven you'" (Mark 2:5). When His authority to forgive sins was challenged by the scribes who were sitting there, He declared, "The Son of Man has power on earth to forgive sins" (Mark 2:10).

It is out of love and compassion that your sins and mine have been forgiven. Because of these mercies it is only our reasonable service to surrender our all to our Lord and Savior. This is what Paul underscores in Romans 12:1, where he writes, "I beseech you therefore, brethren, by the mercies of God, that you present your bodies a living sacrifice, holy, acceptable to God, which is your reasonable service."

As Lord, Christ Alone Has the Right to Possess Us

"To this end Christ died and rose and lived again, that He might be Lord" (v. 9). His living here means the entering into that heavenly life after His human death. By virtue of that resurrection life, He can now penetrate and possess our personalities through the Holy Spirit, and so live again in us.

In certain circumstances there is no more dangerous area than a vacant lot or house. It is the trouble spot for seducers, murderers, robbers, and fornicators. Likewise, there is no more dangerous area in a person's life than the one that is not committed to the sovereignty of Christ. God created men and women to be inhabited, and until the Lord Jesus possesses us, we are open to all manner of satanic attacks.

It was because Peter had refused the way of the cross that he ultimately collapsed under pressure and denied his Master with oaths and curses. Jesus had to turn to him and say, "Get behind Me, Satan! You are an offense to Me, for you are not mindful of the things of God, but the things of men" (Matt. 16:23).

It was because Ananias and Sapphira had not enthroned Jesus as Lord that there was a bridgehead for Satan to enter and fill their hearts with duplicity and deceitfulness. You will remember the searching word to each of them was, "Why has Satan filled your heart to lie to the Holy Spirit and keep back part of the price of the land for yourself? While it remained, was it not your own? And after it was sold, was it not in your own control? Why have you conceived this thing in your heart? You have not lied to men but to God" (Acts 5:3-4).

The Bible gives no hope to any man or woman who does not know Jesus Christ as Lord. As we have observed already, a life that is not possessed by God is open to the control of the Devil. It is only a matter of time before the behavior of that person will manifest the evidences of satanic intrigue and intention. This is why it is so important to state quite categorically that when Jesus Christ possesses us as Lord, He does so with utter completeness;

or to put it in the words of Hudson Taylor: "Jesus Christ is either Lord of all or not Lord at all." To be halfhearted in this matter of personal dedication to the sovereignty of Christ is tantamount to the repudiation of His sovereign authority.

This leads us to consider, in the second place:

THE REALMS OF DIVINE LORDSHIP

"If we live, we live to the Lord; and if we die, we die to the Lord. Therefore, whether we live or die, we are the Lord's" (v. 8). It is plain from these words that in life we are responsible to the lordship of Christ, while in death we are accountable to the lordship of Christ; so that whether we live or die, we can only move within the orbit of the sovereignty of Jesus Christ. Let us look at this a little more closely.

In Life We Are Responsible to the Lordship of Christ

"Christ died and rose and lived again, that He might be Lord of . . . the living" (v. 9). One of the great problems in the church today is that of irresponsible living. It is the result of misinterpreting the doctrine of grace. By preaching cheap grace, we have produced a generation of antinomianists, or lawless ones. Paul, however, makes it plain that one of the functions of the grace of God is to discipline us to deny "ungodliness and worldly lusts [in order that] we should live soberly, righteously, and godly in the present age" (Titus 2:12).

Such grace involves living a life indwelt and controlled by Jesus Christ. Paul says, "I have been crucified with Christ; it is no longer I who live, but Christ lives in me; and the life which I now live in the flesh I live by faith in the Son of God, who loved me and gave

Himself for me" (Gal. 2:20). And then he adds, "I do not set aside the grace of God" (Gal. 2:21). Such a Christ-indwelt life is the utter antithesis of self-centeredness. The question never arises as to what I think, what I speak, or what I do; the issue has been decided once and for all: "No longer I . . . but Christ lives in me" (Gal. 2:20).

In Death We Are Accountable to the Lordship of Christ

"Christ died and rose and lived again, that He might be Lord of . . . the dead" (v. 9). Death is not the cessation of life; it is only a change of life. When a person passes from this scene, he is ushered immediately into the august presence of his Lord. Paul describes this state as being "absent from the body and . . . present with the Lord" (2 Cor. 5:8).

But more than this, there is a day coming when "we must all appear before the judgment seat of Christ, that each one may receive the things done in the body, according to what he has done, whether good or bad" (2 Cor. 5:10). The apostle amplifies this in the passage before us, where he quotes our Lord as saying, "'As I live . . . every knee shall bow to Me, and every tongue shall confess to God.' So then each of us shall give account of himself to God" (Rom. 14:11-12). Before that judgment seat we shall have to answer for service we have rendered, as well as the motivations that have inspired such service. Every life that is lived under the control of the sovereignty of Christ will receive the unqualified "well done" of Jesus Christ. On the other hand, every life that is lived under the mastery of self will suffer unspeakable loss. In the graphic language of 1 Corinthians 3, it will either be "gold, silver, precious stones, [or] wood, hay, straw" (v. 12).

So we see that, whether dead or alive, Jesus Christ must be Lord. That brings us to our third consideration:

Signposts to Guide Us

THE RULES OF DIVINE LORDSHIP

"Christ died and rose and lived again, that He might be Lord" (v. 9). When we examine the context, it is evident to us that Paul has both a prophetic as well as a present application in view when he speaks of every knee bowing and every tongue confessing to God (v. 11). The apostle still has in mind the issues of mutual recognition and personal toleration. This is why he asks, "Why do you judge your brother? Or why do you show contempt for your brother? For we shall all stand before the judgment seat of Christ" (v. 10). The reason, surely, is plain. This matter of submission to the lordship of Christ relates to all aspects of life. There are rules of divine sovereignty, and they are succinctly comprehended in two all-embracing obligations:

*There Must Be Unconditional Submission to Christ
in All Relationships of Life*

"As I live, says the Lord, every knee shall bow to [God]" (v. 11). As we have noted, this is a prophecy of what is going to happen in heaven, on earth, and under the earth in a day yet to come. All angelic hosts will own Christ as Master. Every man, woman, and child will bow to that sovereignty, and even in hell Satan, with all his powers and principalities, will acknowledge that Jesus Christ is Lord, to the glory of God the Father (Phil. 2:9-11). However, there is a present application of this truth, and we need to understand it and then to heed it. Mere talk about the lordship of Christ in some abstract or nebulous fashion is pointless. If Jesus Christ is Lord, then this will be evident in the spheres in which every Christian is to be found.

☐ CHRIST WILL BE LORD IN THE HOME

Addressing husbands and wives, parents and children, Paul says, "submitting to one another in the fear of God" (Eph. 5:21). This calls for the loving submission of the wife to the husband, the loving consideration of the husband to the wife, the loving concern of the parents for the children, and the loving obedience of the children to the parents. Jesus Christ is Lord where these relationships are under the control of a sovereign Lord. If only we knew this in terms of practical experience, all our basic problems in the home would virtually vanish.

☐ CHRIST WILL BE LORD IN THE CHURCH

Speaking to church members, the writer to the Hebrews exhorts, "Obey those who rule over you, and be submissive, for they watch out for your souls, as those who must give account" (Heb. 13:17). Here is an area that is utterly disregarded in most of our churches today. By the infiltration of a false concept of democracy and worldly government, we have nullified God's purpose in the local congregation. The consequences are that we have produced a state of anarchy. Like the days of spiritual declension in the Old Testament times when there was no king in Israel, sadly it has to be stated that "everyone [does] what [is] right in his own eyes" (Judges 17:6). There can be no doubt, however, that God's intention is that the sovereignty of Christ should be recognized in the pastoral leadership of the church, working out through the appointed elders and deacons. Only when such divine authority is respected and obeyed will unity, blessing, and abundant life be enjoyed throughout the membership.

☐ CHRIST WILL BE LORD IN THE STATE

Peter exhorts, "Submit yourselves to every ordinance of man for the Lord's sake, whether to the king as supreme, or to governors, as to those who are sent by him for the punishment of evildoers and for the praise of those who do good" (1 Peter 2:13-14). Every Christian should recognize that there is no power that is not ordained of God. A study of Romans 13 makes this unmistakably clear. In the measure, therefore, in which such authority is in accord with the will of God, the Christian is to comply without complaint or reserve. What a difference this would make in the relationships of the vocational world, the educational world, and the governmental world of our day! This is God's purpose for every life, and we miss the blessing when we fail to submit.

So we see that there can be no question as to what we mean by an unconditional submission to Christ in all the relationships of life.

There Must Be an Unashamed Confession of Christ in All Relationships of Life

"Every tongue shall confess to God" (v. 11). Once again, these words refer to that glorious day when "every knee should bow, of those in heaven, and of those on earth, and of those under the earth, and that every tongue should confess that Jesus Christ is Lord, to the glory of God the Father" (Phil. 2:10-11). In the meantime, we are called upon to glorify our God in the present relationships of life, as we confess the Savior as Lord without shame, sham, or shrinking.

Earlier in the epistle Paul states that if we confess with our mouths the Lord Jesus and believe in our hearts that God has raised Him from the dead, we will be saved (see Rom. 10:9). We must remember, however, that salvation is not only an initial act of God in us, but also a continual activity of God through us. The apostle goes right on to say that the unashamed confession of Christ in all the relationships of life is an outreach of evangelism, even to the ends of the earth. This is why he asks, "How shall they believe in Him of whom they have not heard? And how shall they hear without a preacher? And how shall they preach unless they are sent?" (Rom. 10:14-15). The answer, of course, is that they cannot be sent until Jesus Christ is Lord. So God waits for that redeemed remnant in every age who are going to say and mean, "Jesus Christ is Lord."

Dr. Graham Scroggie was speaking at the Keswick Convention in England on one occasion when he was approached by a young woman who had been greatly stirred by his message on the lordship of Christ. Walking up to him at the close of the service, she said, "I want Jesus Christ to be Lord of my life, but I am afraid God will send me overseas as a missionary, and I don't want to go."

Opening his Bible to Acts 10:14, Dr. Scroggie explained the utter absurdity of Peter's answer. You will remember that God had given Peter a vision of a sheet in which were all manner of four-footed animals, wild beasts, creeping things, and birds of the air. And a voice came to him, "Rise, Peter; kill and eat." But Peter answered, "Not so, Lord!" (see Acts 10:12-14).

The doctor went on to explain, "A slave never dictates to a master." Therefore, to say, 'Not so, Lord,' was impertinent! "Now," advised Dr. Scroggie, "I want you to cross out the two words 'not so' and leave the word 'Lord'; or else cross out the word 'Lord' and leave 'not so.'" Handing her his pencil, he quietly walked away.

For some time she struggled. Then he returned. Looking over her shoulder, he saw a tearstained page. The words "not so" were crossed out. With a glad light in her eyes, she repeated affirmatively, "Lord!" "Lord!" "Lord!" No longer would she dictate. She was now His disciple, and He was her Lord and Master.

Are you prepared to look up into the face of Jesus Christ and say,

> *Lord of every thought and action,*
> *Lord to send and Lord to stay;*
> *Lord in speaking, writing, giving,*
> *Lord in all things to obey;*
> *Now and evermore to be.*
> E. H. SWINSTEAD

Nothing less than this is submission to God's sovereignty.

FOR FURTHER STUDY

1. What was the purpose of our Lord's redemptive work? (See Rom. 14:9.)

2. Why did the author say that yielding to Christ as Lord is the "final solution to all matters of faith and conduct"? Why is such submission reasonable and necessary? (See 1 Cor. 6:20; 1 Peter 1:18-19.)

3. Is it possible to be partly yielded to Christ's lordship? Why or why not?

4. In what practical ways can one make Christ lord in specific

areas of life? Decide on one step you could take to extend Christ's lordship in some aspect of your life.

5. Is the church a democracy? Why or why not? (See Heb. 13:17.) Is *your* church a democracy?

The Signpost of
SPIRIT-FULLNESS

See then that you walk circumspectly, not as fools but as wise, redeeming the time, because the days are evil. Therefore do not be unwise, but understand what the will of the Lord is. And do not be drunk with wine, in which is dissipation; but be filled with the Spirit, speaking to one another in psalms and hymns and spiritual songs, singing and making melody in your heart to the Lord, giving thanks always for all things to God the Father in the name of our Lord Jesus Christ, submitting to one another in the fear of God.

EPHESIANS 5:15-21

6

We live in a day when the doctrine of the person and work of the Holy Spirit in the life of the believer is grossly misunderstood. I believe that one of the devices of the enemy is to carry people to such extremes that they forget the truth that is so balanced and clear in Scripture.

Yet having said that, I believe that one of the greatest needs in the church of Jesus Christ is for a new breath of the Holy Spirit upon it. When the Spirit truly fills a person, the monotonous becomes the momentous, and we enter into the purpose of our Lord Jesus Christ who said, "I have come that they may have life, and that they may have it more abundantly" (John 10:10). Dr. Graham Scroggie used to say, "Every Christian has eternal life, but every Christian does not have abundant life. He may have it potentially, but he may not know it in the fullness of experience."

I want to add to that and say that every true Christian has the indwelling Person of the Spirit, or he wouldn't be a Christian. The Bible says, "If anyone does not have the Spirit of Christ, he is not His" (Rom. 8:9), but it does not follow that every Christian has the fullness of the Spirit. When the apostles wanted to appoint men to serve as deacons in the early church, they looked for individuals who were consciously, continuously, and conspicuously full of the Holy Spirit (see Acts 6:1-7). That was normal Christian living.

With that as a preamble, I want you to consider: first, the truth of the Spirit-filled life; second, the terms of the Spirit-filled life; and third, the test of the Spirit-filled life.

THE TRUTH OF THE SPIRIT-FILLED LIFE

"Be [you being] filled with the Spirit" (5:18) is our text, and Paul reaches this point after dealing with the doctrine of the Holy Spirit in a most exhaustive way throughout this epistle (see 1:3, 13; 2:18; 3:16-17; 4:3; 5:18; 6:17-18). But for our purpose, we shall focus on the verses at the beginning of this chapter. My aim in this study is to deal with the filling of the Holy Spirit. Paul is addressing believers who already knew the incoming, the indwelling, the enabling, and the uniting of the Spirit in their lives, but now he turns to them and says, "Be [you being] filled" (5:18).

The truth of the Spirit-filled life implies a twofold imperative:

The Word of God Commands a Spirit-Filled Life

"Be filled with the Spirit" (5:18). Commenting on this verse, C. H. Spurgeon said, "This is not a promise to claim; this is a command to obey." If sin is disobedience to the revealed Word of God, and I know I ought to be filled with the Spirit but I'm not, then it is sin. For the Bible says, "To him who knows to do good and does not do it, to him it is sin" (James 4:17). So it is not only a matter of whether you have embezzled money or are living with someone else's wife or husband. You could be living in sin because you are not filled with the Holy Spirit, a serious matter indeed!

But not only does the Word of God command it—notice:

Signposts to Guide Us

The Work of God Demands a Spirit-Filled Life

The command to "be filled with the Spirit" (5:18) is applicable to a church setting, "submitting to one another in the fear of God" (5:21). This represents, of course, pastors and people; to a home setting with husbands and wives, parents and children; to a business setting representing masters and servants; to a world setting, a world in which there are "spiritual hosts of wickedness in the heavenly places" (6:12). Right in that context Paul says, "Be filled with the Spirit" (5:18).

If you were to take this text as a lead into the Acts of the Apostles you would find that Peter couldn't preach without being filled with the Holy Spirit (Acts 2:14-36); Stephen couldn't suffer and still praise God without being filled with the Holy Spirit (Acts 7:55-60); Barnabas couldn't exhort without being filled with the Holy Spirit (Acts 11:22-24); and Paul couldn't rebuke without being filled with the Holy Spirit (Acts 13:9-11). The work of God demands it!

When I think of what is being done in the name of Christianity, without the control of the Spirit, my heart trembles. So I want to ask you: In your daily life, are you filled with the Holy Spirit—consciously, continuously, and conspicuously?

THE TERMS OF THE SPIRIT-FILLED LIFE

"And do not be drunk with wine, in which is dissipation; but be filled with the Spirit" (5:18). In words that can be easily understood, the Holy Spirit has outlined the terms for a Spirit-filled life. I want to put them in a simple form and then expound them. First of all, there must be:

The Signpost of Spirit-Fullness

An Initial Acceptance of the Spirit's Control

"Do not be drunk with wine, in which is dissipation" (5:18). Ephesus was a mercantile town, notorious for its drunkenness. It was so bad that even at noonday men could be seen staggering down the streets in a drunken stupor. This is why I believe Timothy was somewhat concerned about taking even a sip of wine for his stomach's sake and his many infirmities (1 Tim. 5:23), for he knew that when a man imbibes liquor, he is controlled.

Paul is drawing a contrast as well as a comparison here. He says, "Do not be drunk with wine, in which is dissipation; but be filled [controlled] with the Spirit" (5:18). He was calling for divine intoxication, not devil-intoxication. The filling of the Spirit is a continuous discipline. So many people seek for the blessings of the Spirit, but it is not a question of getting more of the Spirit, but allowing the Spirit to get more of us.

The story is told of an occasion when D. L. Moody was scheduled to conduct a crusade in a particular city. At one ministers' meeting a young man got up and asked, "Why do we have to have D. L. Moody anyway? After all, does he have a monopoly on the Holy Spirit?" After a quiet pause a saintly pastor rose to his feet and replied, "Young man, Mr. Moody may not have a monopoly on the Holy Spirit, but those of us who know him recognize that the Holy Spirit has a monopoly of him."

There is not only an initial acceptance of the Spirit's control, there must be:

A Continual Dependence on the Spirit's Control

That is the whole meaning of the present tense, "Be [you being] filled with the Spirit" (5:18). As Dr. Handley Moule phrases it, "Let your habitual normal life be that of being constantly filled with the Holy Spirit." You ask, "How can that be maintained?" Two principles will help us here:

☐ *Allegiance to the Lord.* "Understand what the will of the Lord is" (Eph. 5:17). When Christ is truly Lord of the life, the Spirit fills. When Jesus was exalted to the right hand of God the Father, the Holy Spirit was poured out (see Acts 2:33). What happened at Pentecost can happen in personal experience. When He is made Lord of the life, the rivers begin to flow (see John 7:37-39).

But secondly, there must be:

☐ *Obedience to the Word.* The command to "be filled" (5:18) is a divine imperative. And we are reminded elsewhere that the Holy Spirit is "given to those who obey Him" (Acts 5:32). There is no substitute for obedience. "To obey is better than sacrifice, and to heed than the fat of rams" (1 Sam. 15:22). The most important word in all of Christian experience is *obedience*. Even love is meaningless without obedience. Jesus said, "If you love Me, [you will] keep My commandments" (John 14:15). Tell me, is your obedience up to date?

So we have looked at the truth and the terms of the Spirit-filled life, but now consider:

THE TESTS OF THE SPIRIT-FILLED LIFE

"Speaking to one another in psalms and hymns and spiritual songs, singing and making melody in your heart to the Lord . . . submitting to one another in the fear of God. . . . Be strong in the Lord and in the power of His might. Put on the whole armor of God, that you may be able to stand against the wiles of the devil" (Eph. 5:19, 21; 6:10-11). The Ephesian epistle is the full-orbed revelation of truth. Someone has said that this is truth in its totality.

The Signpost of Spirit-Fullness

What is said here is of tremendous importance, both doctrinally and practically.

The tests of the Spirit-filled life will be evident in three areas of life: the church, the home, and the world. When the Christian is Spirit-filled there will be:

Life in the Church

"Speaking to one another in psalms and hymns and spiritual songs, singing and making melody in your heart to the Lord, giving thanks always for all things to God the Father in the name of our Lord Jesus Christ" (5:19-20). Four aspects of worship are described here. There will be:

□ *Spirit-Filled Speaking.* "Speaking to one another in psalms and hymns and spiritual songs" (5:19). This is the expression of God-given truth. This speaking one to another corresponds to the fuller phrase, "teaching and admonishing one another," found in a parallel passage in Colossians 3:16. Whenever we read of Spirit-filled men and women in the Bible, they are always "speaking the truth in love" (Eph. 4:15). In this context it is "teaching and admonishing one another" to engender and enrich worship.

□ *Spirit-Filled Singing.* "Singing and making melody in your heart to the Lord" (5:19). This is the expression of God-given joy. It is a joy unaffected by outside circumstances. Paul and Silas knew this joy when they were "praying and singing hymns to God" in a Roman dungeon (Acts 16:25). When you know how to praise in prison, you have really learned how to "worship [God] in spirit and in truth" (John 4:24).

□ *Spirit-Filled Sharing.* "Giving thanks always for all things to God" (5:20). This is the expression of God-given thanks.

According to 1 Thessalonians 5:18, we are to give thanks in everything, and the writer to the Hebrews adds, "By Him let us continually offer the sacrifice of praise to God, that is, the fruit of our lips, giving thanks to His name" (Heb. 13:15). A thankful heart always issues in a sharing life, and this is what we need more and more in the body of Christ. In thankfulness we share our testimonies, our talents, our tithes, and our time.

☐ *Spirit-Filled Serving.* "Submitting to one another in the fear of God" (5:21). This is the expression of God-given love. Paul reminds us in another place that we should "through love serve one another" (Gal. 5:13). If we know anything of body life, we should be sensitive to one another's needs within the fellowship and respond accordingly. All this and more is part of life in the church.

The Spirit-filled Christian should also demonstrate:

Love in the Home

In chapter 5:22 through 6:4 Paul addresses "wives . . . husbands . . . children" and parents. These verses are a remarkable study in relational love. There is to be:

☐ SUPPORTIVE LOVE

"Wives, submit to [be subject to, reverence] your own husbands, as to the Lord" (5:22). The word *reverence* carries the thought of a worshipful respect. Peter expresses the same thought when he alludes to Sarah who "obeyed Abraham, calling him lord" (1 Peter 3:6). To submit leaves no room for unfaithfulness or double standards. Such an injunction may run contrary to popular trends and modern teaching, but it carries all the authority of heaven nonetheless.

☐ REDEMPTIVE LOVE

Giving this type of love is the role of "husbands" who are to "love [their] wives, just as Christ also loved the church and gave Himself for her" (5:25). This astonishing statement spells out the ultimate in sacrifice. Nothing must stand in the way of a husband's dedication and devotion to his wife. All his behavior in the home should be characterized by chivalry and consideration. Just as the sympathetic nervous system responds to the needs of the human body, so a husband should respond to the spiritual, physical, and material needs of his wife. As prophet, priest, and king in his home, every husband should be responsible for reading the Word of God and leading his family in prayer. Wives and children should be the purer and nobler because of the sanctity of his life and ministry. When a husband is a true lover, there is no problem accepting him as a leader.

☐ PROTECTIVE LOVE

"Fathers [parents], do not provoke your children to wrath, but bring them up in the training and admonition of the Lord" (Eph. 6:4). Parents should demonstrate their love by example, discipline, and precept. Only thus will children be brought up in "the training and admonition of the Lord" (6:4).

☐ RESPONSIVE LOVE

"Children, obey your parents in the Lord, for this is right" (6:1). Children should show their love by obedience and allegiance—obedience until they leave home and allegiance throughout the rest of their lives.

There is no substitute for Spirit-controlled love in the home.

We can attend seminars until our pocketbooks are empty and our patience exhausted, and still fail in our attempt to establish homes for the glory of God. But once the Holy Spirit takes over, interpersonal relationships come together under the sovereignty of Christ in a spirit of love and understanding.

But look again. The impact of a Spirit-filled Christian will be seen by life in the church, love in the home, and:

Light in the World

"Bondservants, be obedient to those who are your masters according to the flesh, with fear and trembling, in sincerity of heart, as to Christ. . . . And you, masters, do the same . . . knowing that your . . . Master also is in heaven, and there is no partiality with Him" (Eph. 6:5-9). Here the apostle issues a call to be:

☐ LIGHT IN THE MARKETPLACE

"With goodwill doing service, as to the Lord, and not to men . . . whether he is a slave or free" (vv. 7-8). The apostle is speaking to servants and masters. Here light is demonstrated by a mutual recognition of each other's rights and roles. When this is done in love, there is no place for insubordination, on the one hand, or injustice on the other. There will be a loving response from servants and also loving respect from masters. The problems of management and labor will find a solution no earthly system of welfare can equal.

☐ LIGHT ON THE BATTLEFIELD

"Be strong in the Lord and in the power of His might. Put on the whole armor of God, that you may be able to stand against the wiles of the devil. . . . Take up the whole armor of God, that you may be able to withstand in the evil day, and having done all, to stand" (6:10-13).

We are living in a day when Satan is on his last rampage and demonic forces are oppressing the church. Among the evils making their incursions in our day are secular humanism, popular syncretism, and regular activism. Sooner or later every Christian will find himself up "against principalities, against powers, against the rulers of the darkness of this age, against spiritual hosts of wickedness in the heavenly places" (6:12). But to be Spirit-filled is to know an answer to every attack of Satan. Only the Spirit can teach the Christian that "the weapons of our warfare are not carnal but mighty in God for pulling down strongholds" (2 Cor. 10:4). We can face and fight the enemy by putting on the whole armor of God, which is Christ in His totality. We fight the enemy by wielding the sword of the Spirit, which is the Word of God, and engaging in prevailing prayer. In Paul's mind, there was no question of defeat for the Spirit-filled Christian. This is why he says in another place, "Thanks be to God, who gives us the victory through our Lord Jesus Christ" (1 Cor. 15:57).

□ LIGHT IN A PRISON CELL

"Praying always . . . for me, that utterance may be given to me, that I may open my mouth boldly to make known the mystery of the gospel, for which I am an ambassador in chains; that . . . I may speak boldly, as I ought to speak" (Eph. 6:18-20). Although these words are more personal and pastoral, they are obviously intended for our edification. The great apostle felt his need of intercessory prayer as he faced a hostile world. He knew that only through the prayers of God's people and the supply of

God's Spirit could he speak with courage and clarity. His burden was to "make known the mystery of the gospel" (6:19). Nothing mattered save his concern to reach men and women with the life-giving message of Christ. Although "an ambassador in chains" (6:20), he wanted to speak boldly—cost what it would! What a man and what a motive! But this was quite impossible without the sufficiency of the Spirit.

The question we need to ask ourselves is simple and straightforward: Is the Holy Spirit filling our lives? Remember, there must be an initial acceptance of His control in our lives. He, and He only, must take over. This is the evidence that we have made Jesus Lord. Then there must be the continual dependence on His control by allegiance to the Lord and obedience to the Word day by day. Oh, to pray and mean:

> *Have Thine own way, Lord!*
> *Have Thine own way!*
> *Hold o'er my being absolute sway!*
> *Fill with Thy Spirit*
> *Till all shall see*
> *Christ only, always,*
> *Living in me!*
>
> ADELAIDE A. POLLARD

FOR FURTHER STUDY

1. Why did Paul tell the Ephesian believers, who already had the indwelling Holy Spirit, to be filled with the Spirit? (Eph. 5:18) Is there any sense in which this verse is optional? Have you treated it as optional?

2. How does a believer get more of the Holy Spirit?

3. What can prevent a Christian from having the fullness of the Spirit? (See Acts 5:32.)

4. What characterizes a church that is experiencing life in the Spirit? How does your church measure up? What characterizes a Spirit-controlled home?

5. Is the Holy Spirit filling your life? How can you tell?

The Signpost of
USEFULNESS

Now as Jesus passed by, He saw a man who was blind from birth. And His disciples asked Him, saying, "Rabbi, who sinned, this man or his parents, that he was born blind?" Jesus answered, "Neither this man nor his parents sinned, but that the works of God should be revealed in him. I must work the works of Him who sent Me while it is day; the night is coming when no one can work. As long as I am in the world, I am the light of the world." When He had said these things, He spat on the ground and made clay with the saliva; and He anointed the eyes of the blind man with the clay. And He said to him, "Go, wash in the pool of Siloam" (which is translated, Sent). So he went and washed, and came back seeing.

JOHN 9:1-7

The Signpost of
USEFULNESS

7

When Paul describes Christian workers who are approved of God for divine service, he says: "If anyone cleanses himself . . . he will be a vessel for honor, sanctified and *useful* for the Master, prepared for every good work" (2 Tim. 2:21). This means that you and I are created, redeemed, and cleansed to be useful in the work of God.

We must regard the work of God as a divine activity. In its origin, operation, and consummation, the work of God is divine. Jesus could say, "My Father has been working until now, and I have been working" (John 5:17); and Paul could add, "We . . . [are] workers together with [God]" (2 Cor. 6:1).

Of all such statements on this subject, however, one of the greatest is here in our text. The Master says, "I must work the works of Him who sent Me while it is day; the night is coming when no one can work" (v. 4). It is both interesting and instructive to observe that the Greek here reads, "We must work the works of Him that sent Me." The Lord Jesus is obviously identifying Himself with His disciples. He is showing them that association with Him in the doing of the work of God is nothing less than divine service. What dignity, liberty, and urgency this brings into our Christian service—wherever it is, at home and abroad. So the Master teaches:

THE DIVINE OBLIGATION
TO BE USEFUL IN SERVICE

"I *must* work the works of Him who sent Me" (v. 4). The person who says that he has no sense of obligation to serve God is a person who has never received the divine nature. "Faith by itself, if it does not have works, is dead" (James 2:17). And Paul declares, "We are His workmanship, created in Christ Jesus for good works, which God prepared beforehand that we should walk in them" (Eph. 2:10). To know a living faith in Christ and to share the divine nature is to be linked with the divine activity of God, both in time and in eternity. This divine obligation expresses itself in a lifelong sense of:

Responsibility to God

"I *must* work the works of *Him who sent Me*" (v. 4). Service for the Lord Jesus Christ was not only important but also imperative.

As I have pointed out in an earlier chapter—as a *Son*, He could say, "I *must* be about My Father's business" (Luke 2:49). Even though subject to Joseph and Mary, He was supremely responsible to His God and Father. The writer to the Hebrews reminds us that "though He was a Son, yet He learned obedience by the things which He suffered" (Heb. 5:8). Oh, that a sense of imperative obedience might come into our lives as sons and daughters of God! This is His purpose in conferring upon us the high privilege of being His children.

As the *Savior*, He could say, "As Moses lifted up the serpent in the wilderness, even so must the Son of Man be lifted up, that whoever believes in Him should not perish but have eternal life" (John 3:14-15). There was a *must* in every aspect of His redemptive work. There was no question of holding back at any point, even though it meant the death of the cross. Note His words as He agonizes in the garden of Gethsemane, "Not My will, but Yours, be done" (Luke 22:42).

There is a very real sense in which God has called us to share the redemptive activity of our Lord Jesus Christ. Needless to say, this does not include the unique and final work He accomplished at Calvary, but it does involve the outworking of the ministry and message of the cross in terms of everyday living and serving. Paul speaks of it as "[filling] up in my flesh what is lacking in the afflictions of Christ, for the sake of His body" (Col. 1:24). Have we accepted this imperative in our Christian service?

Then we notice that as a *servant*, He could say, "I must work the works of Him who sent Me while it is day" (v. 4). As God's perfect bondslave, He made Himself of no reputation, renounced all rights, and even depended on God for daily resources in order to fulfill His perfect will.

The apostle Paul is one of the outstanding examples of identification with Christ in this sense of responsibility in Christian service. He was ever under a sense of burden to fulfill the will of God. He could say, "Necessity is laid upon me; yes, woe is me if I do not preach the gospel!" (1 Cor. 9:16).

This divine obligation involves not only responsibility to God, but also:

Accountability to God

"I must work the works of Him who *sent* Me" (v. 4). The Savior's sense of being *sent* made Him ever aware of His accountability to God. Thus we read that He never spoke anything without its being given Him of God (see John 8:28). Likewise, He never did anything without heaven's permission (see John 5:19, 30). Then, finally, before He returned to heaven, the Master said, "As the Father has sent Me, I also send you" (John 20:21).

We are accountable to God for every word we speak and every work we perform. We cannot afford to act independently of God for one single moment. It is because we have lost this sense of accountability to God that we have become undisciplined and negligent in our Christian service. We have forgotten to recognize that if we are converted, then we are commissioned; if we are saved, then we are sent. Our very oneness with Christ in salvation makes us one with Him in service.

In the next place, we must seize:

THE DIVINE OBJECTIVE TO BE USEFUL IN SERVICE

"I must work the *works* of Him who sent Me" (v. 4). Our Lord leaves us in no doubt as to the ultimate objective in divine service. Not only does He unfold this theme in His teaching throughout this Gospel, but He also dramatically illustrates it in the very context of the chapter we are considering. To put it simply, the divine objective in service implies:

The Personal Receiving of Christ

In chapter 6 of this same Gospel Jesus says, "This is the work of God, that you believe in Him whom He sent" (v. 29). And in chapter 1, verse 12, John defines what is involved in believing when he says, "As many as received Him, to them He gave the right to become children of God, to those who believe in His name." Now this may sound very strange to the ears of people who are so caught up in the frenzy of religious activism that they have no idea as to what Jesus regarded as divine service. No one has the right to lift a little finger in so-called service for God until he or she can claim to have personally received Christ. Thousands of religious people who talk about believing in Christ have never actually received Christ; they know nothing of the indwelling life of Jesus, which, according to the Master, is the first essential in the objective of divine service.

See how this is illustrated in the chapter before us, "'I must work the works of Him who sent Me while it is day; the night is coming when no one can work.' . . . When He had said these things, He spat on the ground and made clay with the saliva; and He anointed the eyes of the blind man with the clay." And we read that the man "came back seeing" (vv. 4, 6-7). Here is a glorious demonstration of the indwelt life. Before Jesus could open the eyes of the blind man and so fulfill the work of God, He had to mix His spittle with earthly clay and anoint the sightless eyes. The *admixture* of the divine spittle with the earthly clay is a dramatic object lesson of the indwelt life.

Before we can open the eyes of blind men and women, we must know what it is to be "partakers of the divine nature" (2 Peter 1:4). Any service done without this genuine experience of personally receiving Christ may be humanly impressive, but it is utterly worthless in the sight of God. This explains why there is so much dearth and death in the life of our churches today.

But with this personal receiving of Christ, the work of God also involves:

The Personal Revealing of Christ

Consider the words of Jesus before He left His disciples: "Most assuredly, I say to you, he who believes in Me, the works that I do he will do also; and greater works than these he will do, because I go to My Father" (John 14:12). If you study the context, you will observe that the supreme work that Jesus came to do was that of revealing His Father. He had just said to Philip, "He who has seen Me has seen the Father" (John 14:9).

Now see this illustrated in the same story that we are considering. Following the miraculous act of healing, the next time Jesus contacts this man is to reveal Himself to him. We read, "[When] Jesus heard that they had cast him out . . . He said to him, 'Do you believe in the Son of God?' He answered and said, 'Who is He, Lord, that I may believe in Him?' And Jesus said to him, 'You have both seen Him and it is He who is talking with you.' Then he said, 'Lord, I believe!' And he worshiped Him" (John 9:35-38).

Needless to say, we cannot personally reveal Christ until we have received Christ, but if there is a genuine experience of the indwelling Savior, then we have a supreme responsibility to reveal Christ consciously, conspicuously, and continually in every area of life.

We have been so indoctrinated to think of Christian service as this work or that work, until we have been corrupted from the simplicity that is in Christ. A housewife revealing Christ to her children is as much in full-time Christian service as an evangelist who proclaims the Gospel to thousands. A businessman revealing Christ in his office is as much in divine service as the missionary blazing the trail for Christ on the foreign field.

God has no other reason for leaving us on this earth after our conversion, unless it is to serve Him in the winning and discipling of souls. Our spheres of activity may be as varied as the number of Christians in this world, but the objective is ever the same. For some, the pulpit may be the Christian home; for others, an office in the city; for many, it will be the university campus; for a precious few, the uttermost part of the earth. But, ultimately, there is only one objective—the completion of the body of Christ through every-member evangelism. How we earn our bread and butter is secondary; the primary call is to the same objective that motivated our blessed Savior: "I must work the works of Him who sent Me" (v. 4).

In the third place, notice:

THE DIVINE OPPORTUNITY TO BE USEFUL IN SERVICE

"I must work the works of Him who sent Me *while it is day*" (v. 4). A sense of urgency characterized our Lord in everything He said and did. Indeed, He taught and demonstrated by His life two important principles in regard to the matter of opportunity:

All Time Must Be Utilized Redemptively

"I must work the works of Him who sent Me while it is day" (v. 4). Jesus worked to a timetable and, therefore, never wasted a moment. In this respect He was never caught off guard.

Recall, for instance, the occasion when His own mother prematurely asked Him to perform a miracle, and He replied with gentle insistence, "Woman, what does your concern have to do with Me? My hour has not yet come" (John 2:4). And then again at the end of His ministry, He could say, "For this purpose I came to this hour" (John 12:27); and still again, "The hour has come" (John 12:23).

The Signpost of Usefulness

No one has ever been great or useful, in the highest sense, who has not regarded time in a similar manner. The following lines are inscribed on a clock in Chester Cathedral in England:

> *When as a child I laughed and wept,*
> *Time crept.*
> *When as a youth I dreamt and talked,*
> *Time walked.*
> *When I became a full-grown man,*
> *Time ran.*
> *When older still I daily grew,*
> *Time flew.*
> *Soon I shall find on travelling on—*
> *Time gone!*

So may God "teach us to number our days, that we may gain a heart of wisdom" (Ps. 90:12), or to put it in the language of the New Testament, let us redeem "the time, because the days are evil" (Eph. 5:16).

From the Savior's words in our text, two important facts impinge upon our use of time redemptively:

☐ THE BREVITY OF THE DAY OF SERVICE

Jesus said, "I must work the works of Him who sent Me while it is day; the night is coming when no one can work" (v. 4). "The time is short" (1 Cor. 7:29). Before we know it, the night will come, and our day of opportunity will be gone forever.

☐ THE URGENCY OF THE DAY OF SALVATION

The Master declared, "As long as I am in the world, I am the light of the world" (John 9:5). What a reminder that the day of salvation will one day end without warning. Paul puts it plainly when he exclaims, "Behold, *now* is the accepted time; behold, *now* is the day of salvation" (2 Cor. 6:2). When the door is shut, it is shut forever!

The second principle regarding this matter of opportunity is that:

All Toil Must Be Organized Redemptively

"*I must work the works* of Him who sent Me" (v. 4). The Lord Jesus gave His all, and so must we. The language of the apostle must ever characterize our availability for God: "So, as much as is in me, I am *ready* to preach the gospel" (Rom. 1:15). The adjective *ready* means eager, willing, organized (note Mark 14:38: "The spirit indeed is willing [or truly is *ready*], but the flesh is weak"). The great commentator Swete says that the spirit's "willingness was not a match for the inertia of its colleague, the frail flesh." We can never serve God with wholehearted faithfulness until we are redemptively organized. Or to put it in the words of a lovely hymn:

> All for Jesus, all for Jesus!
> All my being's ransomed pow'rs:
> All my tho'ts and words and doings,
> All my days and all my hours.
> MARY D. JAMES

So we have seen what we mean by useful service. First, there must be the divine obligation: A sense of imperative must come into our lives as we share the life of Christ. With that obligation must come a divine objective—the evangelization of the world. And last, but not least, we must know something of this divine opportunity. God has given us today. Tomorrow may never come. One of the most solemn realizations that can come to a

Christian is that he can miss God's day of opportunity. Let us remember that Paul was addressing Christians when he wrote, "Behold, now is the accepted time; behold, now is the day of salvation" (2 Cor. 6:2). So may we bring our time and talents and say, with deep responsiveness:

> *O use me, Lord, use even me,*
> *Just as Thou wilt, and when, and where;*
> *Until Thy blessed face I see,*
> *Thy rest, Thy joy, Thy glory share*
> FRANCES R. HAVERGAL

FOR FURTHER STUDY

1. The author refers to the work of God (of your church) as a divine activity. Is that the way you view it? What can you do as a church member to allow the Holy Spirit to do His work more freely in your midst?

2. For what were you created? (See Eph. 2:10.) Assess where you are in the process of fulfilling this purpose. What is essential in order to be linked with the divine activity of God?

3. Describe the model for Christian service done in collaboration with God. (See John 5:19, 30; 8:28.)

4. Of what does the work of God consist—"the works of Him who sent Me"? (See John 6:29; John 9:4, 6, 7; Acts 10:38; John 20:21.)

5. How do your use of time and your set of priorities affect your service for God?

The Signpost of
READINESS

✳

"But when you see Jerusalem surrounded by armies, then
know that its desolation is near. Then let those who are in
Judea flee to the mountains, let those who are in the midst of
her depart, and let not those who are in the country enter her.
For these are the days of vengeance, that all things which are
written may be fulfilled. But woe to those who are pregnant
and to those who are nursing babies in those days! For there
will be great distress in the land and wrath upon this people.
And they will fall by the edge of the sword, and be led away
captive into all nations. And Jerusalem will be trampled by
Gentiles until the times of the Gentiles are fulfilled. And there
will be signs in the sun, in the moon, and in the stars; and on
the earth distress of nations, with perplexity, the sea and the
waves roaring; men's hearts failing them from fear and the
expectation of those things which are coming on the earth, for
the powers of the heavens will be shaken. Then they will see
the Son of Man coming in a cloud with power and great glory.
Now when these things begin to happen, look up and lift up
your heads, because your redemption draws near." Then He
spoke to them a parable: "Look at the fig tree, and all the trees.
When they are already budding, you see and know for yourselves that summer is now near. So you also, when you see
these things happening, know that the kingdom of God is near.

Assuredly, I say to you, this generation will by no means pass away till all things take place. Heaven and earth will pass away, but My words will by no means pass away. But take heed to yourselves, lest your hearts be weighed down with carousing, drunkenness, and cares of this life, and that Day come on you unexpectedly. For it will come as a snare on all those who dwell on the face of the whole earth. Watch therefore, and pray always that you may be counted worthy to escape all these things that will come to pass, and to stand before the Son of Man."

LUKE 21:20-36

READINESS

8

The context in which our reading occurs is known as the Olivet Discourse, that prophetic pronouncement that our Lord Jesus Christ made before He went to the cross. It is recorded almost in its entirety in the Synoptic Gospels (Matthew, Mark, and Luke). In answer to a question His disciples had raised, the Lord Jesus used history, prophecy, and imagery to emphasize the importance and imminence of His ultimate return to earth.

In terms of *history,* the disciples were discussing the temple with its high walls, its golden dome, its magnificent splendor, and the massiveness of its stones. Yet Jesus predicted the destruction of this remarkable edifice, and true to His word, it happened. In A.D. 70 the entire temple was razed to the ground.

Prophecy deals with events yet to be fulfilled, but somehow prophecy is becoming history, even today. In verses 20-28 Jesus lists some of the signs that will precede His return to earth—"signs in the sun, in the moon, and in the stars; and on the earth distress of nations, with perplexity, the sea and the waves roaring; men's hearts failing them from fear . . . the powers of the heavens . . . shaken." Some scholars say that the references to sun, moon, and stars represent dominions, powers, and thrones. Others believe it refers to astronomical signs that will be evident as our Lord's coming draws near. Even now we are seeing the beginnings of these signs; prophecy is becoming history. That word *perplexity* is a Greek term that means "no way out." How well that describes nations at their wits' end.

From history and prophecy we move to *imagery*. Verses 29-33 deal with what is happening in Israel today—the budding of the fig tree. Nothing has been more exciting in this century than to witness the birth of Israel and to see the important role she is playing on the world's stage.

Against that backdrop our Savior ends this twenty-first chapter with a clarion call to Christian alertness. He reminds us of:

THE DAY THAT WE ARE TO ANTICIPATE

"Take heed . . . lest . . . that Day come on you unexpectedly" (v. 34). That Day is coming—of that there is no doubt. Our Lord says that Day will be characterized by two things:

The Day Will Come Stealthily

"Take heed to yourselves, lest your hearts be weighed down . . . and that Day come on you unexpectedly" (v. 34). This is the picture of a thief who breaks into a house with the owners unaware. It is the stealthiness of a mugger who silently and slyly approaches an unsuspecting victim. Our Lord is using a figure of speech to describe life. The dawn of each new day is not heralded by some tremendous trumpet blast; instead, it tiptoes into our consciousness. Hours later, "shadows of the evening steal across the sky," as the hymnist puts it, giving way to nightfall. Look at age. Yesterday you were a child, then a teenager. You entered adulthood, and before you knew it, you were a senior citizen. Life has a way of creeping up on you unawares.

The Day Will Come Suddenly

"Take heed to yourselves, lest . . . that Day come on you . . . as a snare" (vv. 34-35). Godet and Alexander Maclaren, in their commentaries, point out that the image here is of an individual who hunts birds for sport. The fowler walks out into a field, hides behind a tree or rock, and watches as the birds come down to feed. At first they are alert, but, sensing no danger, they become absorbed in picking up the grain. Suddenly the fowler lifts his net and with one quick stroke swoops down to trap his bird. That is the picture behind that word *snare*.

For years the subject of the Lord's return was the hobbyhorse of ministers and evangelists alike. They discussed prophetic truth from every angle; yet nowadays people become so absorbed in their own programs that they are in danger of forgetting the urgency and challenge of the message they preach. If they persist on their course, that Day will come upon them unawares.

THE DANGERS THAT WE ARE TO AVOID

"Take heed to yourselves, lest your hearts be weighed down with carousing, drunkenness, and cares of this life" (v. 34). Three distinct dangers are mentioned here—eating, drinking, and working.

The Dissipations of Life

"Take heed to yourselves, lest your hearts be weighed down with carousing" (v. 34). One of our favorite pastimes is eating. It could well be said of us, as it was of the Cretes, "whose god is their belly" (Phil. 3:19). Our Savior is not referring to gluttony, though that may be included. It relates, rather, to that which symbolizes the dissipations of life.

The Signpost of Readiness

Someone has estimated that in an average lifetime of seventy years, a person spends six years eating. Measure that against the time spent reading the Word of God! When our Lord talked about surfeiting, He was thinking of an Eastern meal that could last anywhere from six hours to three weeks! As Christian people, we need to be alert. It is so easy to be caught up in the spirit of the age.

An anonymous author, who chose to live for the fleeting things of this world, penned the following lines in great remorse: "How foolishly I have employed myself! In what delirium has my life been passed! How I've wasted my life while the sun in its race and the stars in their courses have lent their beams—perhaps only to light me to perdition! I have pursued shadows and entertained myself with dreams. I have been treasuring up dust and sporting myself with the wind. I might have grazed with the beasts of the fields or sung with the birds of the woods to much better purposes than any for which I have lived!"

The Stimulations of Life

"Take heed to yourselves, lest your hearts be weighed down with . . . drunkenness" (v. 34). The late Professor Arnold Toynbee has pointed out that one of the indications that a nation is on its way to ruin is a craze for excitement. Why do people drink? It is a stimulant. Yet what many fail to realize is that what starts out as a stimulant usually ends up as a sedative. The whole idea of drunkenness is symbolized by this craze for excitement, where people need one kick after another. If it is not alcohol, then it is drugs, sex, sports to excess, or some other habit, until we are "drunk."

Christian, what do you need to keep you stimulated? What is it you long for most? It is amazing how addicted we can become to things that are legitimate in themselves, but that can end up mastering us until we become enslaved.

A story in one of the *McGuffey's Readers* tells of a miser who had a secret basement where he had hoarded large sums of silver and gold. He came often to look over the money and to run his bony fingers through the coins. But one day a strong wind blew the door shut to his secret basement. A spring lock (that could be turned only from the outside) fastened the door. The miser was shut in with his gold and his god. Years later when the old house was being torn down, some men came across his skeleton stretched out over the silver and gold. He had made money his god, and the god had finally destroyed him.

In our society idolatry is not so much a matter of making gods of wood and stone. We tend to worship gods of chrome, steel, and glass (automobiles, houses, antiques, 31-inch color TV screens, etc.). Our generation is steeped in idolatry; only it is a "respectable" idolatry, instead of a heathen idolatry. It is a polished form of idolatry instead of a crude form.[1]

The Occupations of Life

"Take heed to yourselves, lest your hearts be weighed down with . . . cares" (v. 34). The word *cares* means "to draw in different directions" or "that which causes anxieties." Generally speaking, this includes the occupations of life. God's ideal for man was healthy occupation. Indeed, the Bible says, "If anyone will not work, neither shall he eat" (2 Thess. 3:10). Scripture teaches that work is one of the greatest gifts of God to man. Adam, in his innocence in the garden of Eden, was given a job to do (see Gen. 2:15).

Inherent within the human personality is a God-given creativity, but carried to excess, we become workaholics and subject to occupational neuroses and burnout. The cares of this world, which God never intended us to carry, press in upon us until we can hardly breathe. This is not restricted to busy executives; it can be right at the heart of the ministry. It is possible for God's servants to be intensely overworked doing the Lord's work. We need to "beware of the barrenness of a busy life!" Or as a great Bible teacher in Britain once put it, "Beware lest service sap spirituality." The danger is that Christian service can become religious activism until, ultimately, it smothers us. Therefore, let us maintain a Christian alertness.

THE DUTIES THAT WE ARE TO ASSUME

"Watch therefore, and pray always that you may be counted worthy to escape all these things that will come to pass, and to stand before the Son of Man" (v. 36). The Lord could have outlined a whole list of instructions for us to follow as we await His return, but He summed it up in two words—*watchfulness* and *prayerfulness*. He was constantly using the terms *watch, pray,* and *work* in eschatological passages and parables, as if those constituted the three main duties of the Christian (which they are!).

Watchfulness

"Watch therefore" (v. 36). This word suggests three other thoughts that must be touched on briefly:

☐ EXPECTANCY

"Looking for the blessed hope" (Titus 2:13). Every Christian should be on the tiptoe of expectancy, as if the Lord Jesus were coming today. Ultimately, we are going to be judged on whether or not we have "loved His appearing" (2 Tim. 4:8) and have awaited His return with expectancy. If we have, then we shall receive a reward (2 Tim. 4:8).

☐ TRANSPARENCY

"Everyone who has this hope in Him purifies himself, just as He is pure" (1 John 3:3). Expectancy leads to transparency. No one can live in the Advent light without being transparent before God. Such transparency means walking in the light of openness to the Lord and obedience to the Word day by day (1 John 1:7).

☐ ACTIVITY

"For we were saved in this hope, but hope that is seen is not hope; for why does one still hope for what he sees? But if we hope for what we do not see, we eagerly wait for it with perseverance" (Rom. 8:24-25). The poet Milton wrote, "They also serve who only stand and wait." Watching is not loafing; watching is serving. That thought is wonderfully underscored in 2 Peter 3:12 where the Greek indicates that activity actually hastens the day of God by being busy in His service. It is not simply work for the Lord, but the work of the Lord (1 Cor. 15:58).

Someday you may visit the interesting and historic French-Canadian city of Quebec. There you will see the Plains of Abraham, where the English forces of General Wolfe won Quebec from the French. When you see the steep ascent that Wolfe's men made up the face of the great rocky cliffs, you will be amazed that they succeeded. Mere boys should have been able to hold off a force of soldiers from scaling such cliffs and gaining the heights. Yet Wolfe and his men made the ascent and gained the citadel. Why? Because the overconfident defenders became careless and pleasure-loving. One night, when they were off guard, the enemy saw their opportunity, scaled the heights, and took the city. Quebec fell because its defenders failed to keep watch. And, for failure to keep watch, thousands are losing the battles of life every day, while at the last for failure to keep watch, many will be unready for the return of Jesus Christ.[2]

Prayerfulness

"Pray always that you may be counted worthy to escape all these things that will come to pass, and to stand before the Son of Man" (v. 36). Even though these words are spoken primarily to that remnant that will await the coming of our Lord in all His power and glory, the principle applies equally to us today.

☐ THERE MUST BE CONTINUOUS PRAYER

"Pray always" (v. 36). The Savior emphasized the importance of prayer when He declared, "Men always ought to pray and not lose heart" (Luke 18:1). The *ought* there is a word without moods. It is not subject to feelings, circumstances, or rationalizations. We owe it to God to pray; we owe it to ourselves, our church, and to a dying world. Not to pray is to faint, and when we faint, we relax in body. One of the most glib expressions we use is: "Take it easy" or "Relax." The trouble is, we relax on anything else but prayer! We wouldn't think of missing out on things we consider priority, but announce a prayer meeting, and that is our night off! Paul also challenges us concerning this matter of continuous prayer. He urges us, "Pray without ceasing," and again, "Praying always with all prayer and supplication in the Spirit, being watchful to this end with all perseverance and supplication for all the saints" (1 Thess. 5:17; Eph. 6:18).

Signposts to Guide Us

☐ THERE MUST BE VICTORIOUS PRAYER

"That you may be counted worthy to escape all these things that will come to pass, and to stand before the Son of Man" (v. 36). Unless we know how to bend our knees before God, we will never stand upright before Him in a coming day. A ministry without prayer is futile. A soul-winning ministry without prayer is fruitless. Only victorious prayer will overcome temptation, seduction, the allurements of the world, and one's own inertia.

Luther once remarked, "I am so busy now that I find if I did not spend two or three hours each day in prayer, I could not get through the day. If I should neglect prayer but a single day, I should lose a great deal of the fire of faith."[3]

Here, then, is the call to Christian alertness. God is speaking to us. There is a day we are to anticipate. Stealthily and suddenly it will be upon us. There are the dangers we are to avoid—those dissipations, stimulations, and consuming occupations of life. There are the duties that we are to assume with an expectancy, transparency, and activity that please the Savior and a prayerfulness that is continuous and victorious. Let us take heed. Let us be alert and awake to His coming. Jesus could very well come today!

> *It may be at morn, when the day is awaking,*
> *When sunlight through darkness and shadow is breaking,*
> *That Jesus will come in the fullness of glory*
> *To receive from the world His own.*
>
> *O Lord Jesus, how long, how long*
> *Ere we shout the glad song—*
> *Christ returneth! Hallelujah!*
> *Hallelujah, amen, Hallelujah, amen.*
>   H. L. TURNER

FOR FURTHER STUDY

1. What are some things in our lives that can crowd God out? Are any of these a problem for you? If so, what will you do about it?

2. Where is the line between Christian service and religious activism? How do you find the balance between being and doing?

3. What does the author list as the three main duties of Christians? How are you fulfilling these duties?

4. Is it possible to carry out Paul's instruction in 1 Thessalonians 5:17? Explain your answer. Relate anything that has helped you in this area.

5. Why do Christians need to be ready?

CONCLUSION

The teachings presented in this book "have a history." They represent an approach to the Christian life expounded by some of the church's most illustrious leaders—R. A. Torrey, Donald Barnhouse, Paul Rees, A. J. Gordon, G. Campbell Morgan, E. M. Blaiklock—to name only a few. Their platform was the annual Keswick Convention that began meeting in England in the late 1800s.

Few events have had a greater impact on the church or influenced more people to go deeper in the Christian walk than the Keswick movement. With lives transformed by the message of scriptural holiness, men and women volunteered for the mission field, entered the ministry, and became leaders of Christian organizations. Thousands of those touched at Keswick went on, in turn, to minister to tens of thousands of others all over the world—people such as Betty Stam (martyred in China), Amy Carmichael, Hudson Taylor, C. T. Studd.

Modern evangelicals have a great and godly heritage, to which Keswick contributed an important part. We include a little of the story of Keswick because we believe that seeing the message of holiness in the context of this movement's unique influence can give readers a deeper appreciation of these truths.

THE PUBLISHER

Conclusion

The foregoing chapters by no means exhaust the critical issues in our walk with Christ, but they do cover the basic themes that have dominated the teaching at the yearly Keswick Conventions held in many parts of the world. The "mother" Keswick convenes every year during the month of July in a little town called Keswick, which nestles on the foot of Skiddaw Mountain and beside beautiful Lake Derwentwater, in the Lake District of northern England. It is a region made famous by its association with the Lake poets—Wordsworth, Coleridge, and Southey—and it is known for its picturesque and fascinating scenery.

Since 1875, when the first convention was held, the influence of "Keswick teaching" has been increasingly felt in the Christian world, until it has come to be regarded as one of the most potent spiritual forces in recent church history.

Dr. Steven Barabas (now deceased), former Professor of Theology at Wheaton College, wrote faithfully and objectively on the Keswick movement. His book is called *So Great Salvation—The History and Message of the Keswick Convention.*[1] In his chapters on the sequence of teaching at Keswick, he outlines with careful elaboration: 1) The Exceeding Sinfulness of Sin, 2) God's Provision for Sin, 3) Consecration, 4) The Spirit-filled Life, and 5) Christian Service. This progressive teaching took shape because it was observed that believers generally pass through these successive stages or crises of experience as they pursue scriptural holiness and Spirit-fullness.

In his foreword to the book, Fred Mitchell, then chairman of the Keswick Convention Council (1948–51), concludes with a "fair comment" statement: "Some will necessarily criticize the book, as Keswick itself has been and still is criticized, but that is of no serious consequence. The truth of God is bigger than any one view or school of thought. If other theologies of holiness help some others to be holy more than Keswick, then we rejoice; but Dr. Barabas's book will certainly help many to experience more fully the 'so great salvation' which grace has provided, and which is waiting for the appropriation of faith."

Among the untold number of those who have appropriated "the so great salvation" Dr. Barabas cites these well-known individuals (known especially by their writings):

Andrew Murray (1828–1917)

About the year 1820, the Dutch Reformed Church of South Africa, alarmed at the spread of rationalism in its midst and distrusting the clergymen that came from Holland, sent a sharp cry to Scotland for some godly ministers to come to them with the Gospel. One of those who responded was Andrew Murray the First, who had received his college education at Aberdeen and, before going to South Africa, studied theology at Utrecht in the Dutch tongue. His labours and his zeal were apostolic. He married a South African Dutch girl, by whom he had seventeen children, of whom Andrew Murray the Second, the subject of this sketch, was one.

Andrew and his older brother, John, who later became professor of theology at Stellenbosch, like their father before them, went to Aberdeen and Utrecht for their schooling. Andrew was only twenty when he returned to South Africa. For seven years he worked as a missionary to the Orange Free State and the Transvaal, a parish about twice the size of England. In 1860 he accepted a call to Worcester, eighty miles from Cape Town; from there he went to Cape Town; and from Cape Town to Wellington, where he laboured from 1871 to the end of his life.

Conclusion

Dr. Murray was present at Keswick for the first time in 1882, not on the platform, but in the audience. Here is a testimony from his own lips.

On Tuesday evening, at the after-meeting, I rose with others to testify my desire, but could not rise a second time with those who could testify that they had realized that Christ was to them what they had believed. It was as if I only felt how utterly helpless every effort to grasp the blessing is, and could do nothing but bow in emptiness before the Lord. On Wednesday evening I was again in the after-meeting, and it was there the Lord revealed Himself. And as the words of the simple chorus were sung—"wonderful cleansing, wonderful filling, wonderful keeping"—I saw it all, Jesus cleansing, Jesus filling, Jesus keeping.

I had for a year back been seeing what wonderful things God's word says about the power of the blood of Christ. It was "through the blood" that the God of peace brought again from the dead our Lord Jesus. It was by His own blood He entered into the holy place. It was with the blood of the better sacrifice that the heavenly things themselves were purged. It was thus through the blood that the power of sin and death had been overcome, through the blood alone that Christ had obtained and could hold His place in heaven as our Mediator. The blood had obtained such mighty victories in the kingdom of sin and hell, and in the kingdom of heaven, too. Surely that blood that could cleanse the soul is a power but too little known.

I believed and I received Jesus as my Cleanser. I looked to Him to make the blood-sprinkling as glorious and effectual as the blood-shedding was. And I saw that the filling cannot but follow the cleansing. The vessel He hath cleansed He will not leave empty; the temple He hath cleansed, He will fill with His glory.

I could say more, but this is enough just to give my grateful testimony to the love of our blessed Lord, and what He has done for me at Keswick.*

---

*"The Life of Faith," *Keswick Week* (October 2, 1882), 221.

Handley C. G. Moule (1841–1920)

Among the many leaders in the spiritual life who joined the Keswick group in the latter half of the 1880s was H. C. G. Moule, then Principal of Ridley Hall, Cambridge.

He was born in 1841 at Fordington, near Dorchester, where his father was vicar. All seven boys in the family who grew up to maturity achieved distinction. At Cambridge University J. B. Lightfoot was Handley's first college tutor and lecturer. Later Moule said of him:

> No man ever loitered so late in the Great Court that he did not see Lightfoot's lamp burning in his study window; and the most regular worshipper in morning chapel at seven o'clock always found Lightfoot there with him. . . . His strong points were unfailing thoroughness of knowledge and unsurpassable clearness of exposition and instruction. Great was my sense of loss when, in 1861, he resigned his tutorship to become Hulsean Professor of Divinity.*

---

*J. B. Harford and F. C. Macdonald, *Handley Carr Glyn Moule, Bishop of Durham. A Biography* (London: Hodder and Stoughton, 1922), 18-19.

At college (Trinity) he won various Latin and Greek prizes, and in the Classical Tripos Examination his name appeared sec-

Conclusion

ond in the First Class. The next year he took a First Class in his theological examination and became a Fellow of Trinity.

For four years he was a Master at Marlborough, and then for five years he worked with his father, as his curate. In 1873 he returned to Cambridge to become first Junior, then Senior Dean. In 1880 he became the first Principal of Ridley Hall, a new theological college of the Evangelical School, the counterpart of which at Oxford was Wycliffe Hall, opened three years before. He was Principal of Ridley Hall for eighteen years, and then became Norrisian Professor of Divinity at Cambridge University, which post he left in 1901 to become Bishop of Durham. His immediate predecessors in the See of Durham were Lightfoot and Westcott, and it was universally thought that he was no unworthy successor of these great scholars. This position he held until his death in 1920.

The year before he died Bishop Moule, in an address delivered at Keswick, told the story of his regeneration and entrance into the Keswick movement in the following words:

> I first take you back just fifty-two years, to the time when I began to understand and possess some of the possessions which Keswick loves to show us the way to. In the year 1867, at twenty-five, my mother led me to the Lord Jesus Christ. I had a good post as a form-master in a great public school. I was very well satisfied with life. To a certain extent, with all sorts of internal contradictions to the feeling, I was fairly satisfied with myself. And God in His great mercy kept me from what would be called wrong life, though not from a world of evil within.
>
> Then, one quiet day, I know not in the least how, nor shall I know in this life, there came on me conviction of sin, in its old-fashioned form, a sight of how richly I

deserved the wrath of God and banishment from Him forever, for I had kept Him out of my heart. With almost a fire in my brain I went to my mother. I will not dwell upon her holy memory. Enough to say that she led me with God-given wisdom to the feet of Jesus and by spirit-sight I saw the Lamb upon the Cross of Calvary, and knew that He and only He stood between me and the second death.

All this was [many] years ago, dear friends in Christ . . . but it is to me as if yesterday. What have I to say as to the time since then? Has it been unbroken victory—has it been unbroken rest? No. By whose fault? Never the Master's. Every day and every hour He has been as full of help as ever; He has been as close at hand as ever. But did I never get indolent in the use of His helps to keeping awake? Did I never let myself get slack about regular prayer, when there was no excuse for slackness? Did I never let myself get careless over search of the Bible? Did I never let myself get indifferent about little bits of unpretending duty? Inevitably then something seemed as if it paralysed the fingers that were to use the Lord. And the Lord, unused, humbled the man again and again, letting him feel what it would all be again if he did not possess his possessions and use what he possessed.

But I know this well, that to this day, through these long years, with a Church and a world changed, with my life changed, as many a joy and many a sorrow has come over it, while God has often broken up the ground under my feet and clouded the sky above my head, and has put me to some of the greatest tests that human loss can bring, while also crowning me with mercies—all I can say is that, just as the old secret is used, the surrender of the spirit to the Lord, the same delightful results are assured, because He is the same. There is still a rest and a power for the soul, which means nothing less than this wonderful Christ for me now, in this after-blessing, as I ought to have seen Him from the first. Christ is still in me to make the weak strong, to make the easily defeated Christian conqueror, through Him that loved us.*

---

*H. C. G. Moule, *Christ and the Christian* (London: Marshall Bros., Ltd., 1919), 49-58.

F. B. Meyer (1847–1929)

F. B. Meyer was the best-known Baptist clergyman of his day. It is doubtful, indeed, whether any other minister of his time was better known throughout the world. Although an active pastor all his life to within a few years of his death, he traveled all over the world on preaching missions, making twelve journeys to America alone.

He was born in London, in 1847, and after preparing for the gospel ministry at Regent's Park College, was graduated from London University. He held pastorates at York, Leicester, and London—all of them notable ones. Twice he was President of the National Free Church Council, and once, President of the Baptist Union.

Like Andrew Murray he was a prolific author, writing literally scores of books, in every field of Christian literature, many of which are still in print. His books are not of a very scholarly nature, but all are carefully written and dependable, evincing not only an unusual talent for fluent writing, but rare spiritual insight as well.

Dr. Meyer was present at the famous Broadlands, Oxford, and Brighton Conventions, and could tell of light and help that had come to him in each of these gatherings; but a visit of two members of the famous "Cambridge Seven"—Stanley Smith and C. T. Studd—to Leicester in 1885, when they were the guests of Dr.

Meyer, was the incident that led to a definite step in his experience that finally equipped him to take his place on the Keswick platform. Let us allow him to tell the story in his own words:

> The visits of Messrs. Stanley Smith and Studd to Melbourne Hall will always mark an epoch in my own life. Before then my Christian life was spasmodic and fitful; now flaming up with enthusiasm, and then pacing wearily over leagues of grey ashes and cold cinders. I saw that these young men had something which I had not, but which was within them a constant source of rest and strength and joy. And never shall I forget a scene at 7 A.M. in the grey November morning, as daylight was flickering into the bedroom, paling the guttered candles which from a very early hour had been lighting up the page of Scripture and revealing the figures of the devoted Bible students, who wore the old cricketing or boating costume of earlier days, to render them less sensible of the raw, damp climate. The talk we held then was one of the most formative influences of my life. Why should I not do what they had done? Why should I not yield my whole nature to God, working out day by day that which He would will and work within? Why should I not be a vessel, though only of earthenware, meet for the Master's use, because purged and sanctified?
>
> There was nothing new in what they told me. They said that "a man must trust Him for victory over every sin, and for deliverance from every care." They said that "the Lord Jesus was willing to abide in the heart which was wholly yielded up to Him." They said that "if there were some things in our lives that made it difficult for us to surrender our whole nature to Christ, yet if we were willing to be made willing to surrender them, He would make us not only willing but glad." They said that "directly we give or attempt to give ourselves to Him, He takes us." All this was simple enough. I could have

Conclusion

said it myself. But they urged me to take the definite step; and I shall be forever thankful that they did. And if in a distant country they should read this page, let them be encouraged to learn that one heart at least has been touched with a new fire, and that one voice is raised in prayer for their increase in the knowledge and love of Him who has become more real to the supplicant, because of their brotherly words.

Very memorable was the night when I came to close quarters with God. The Angel that wrestled with Jacob found me, eager to make me a Prince. There were things in my heart and life which I felt were questionable, if not worse; I knew that God had a controversy with respect to them; I saw that my very dislike to probe or touch them was a clear indication that there was mischief lurking beneath. It is the diseased joint that shrinks from the touch and tender eye that shudders at the light. At the same time I did not feel willing to give these things up. It was a long struggle. At last I said feebly, "Lord, I am willing to be made willing; I am desirous that Thy will should be done in me and through me, as thoroughly as it is done in Heaven; come and take me and break me and make me." *That was the hour of crisis, and when it had passed, I felt able at once to add, "And now I give myself to Thee* [italics added]: body, soul and spirit; in sorrow or in joy; in the dark or in the light; in life or in death, to be Thine only, wholly and forever. Make the most of me that can be made for Thy glory." No rapture or rush of joy came to assure me that the gift was accepted. I left the place with almost a heavy heart. I simply assured myself that He must have taken that which I had given, and at the moment of my giving it. And to that belief I clung in all the days that followed, constantly repeating to myself the words, "I am His." And thus at last the joy and rest entered and victory and freedom from burdening care, and I found that He was moulding my will and making it easy to do what I had thought impossible; and I felt that He was leading me into the paths of righteousness for His name's sake, but so gently as to be almost imperceptible to my weak sight.*

---

*W. Y. Fullerton, *F. B. Meyer, A Biography* (London: Marshall, Morgan & Scott, Ltd., n.d.), 57-58.

To these testimonies we as the publisher would add Stephen Olford's own powerful testimony, as told by Dr. John Phillips in his biography *Only One Life: The Biography of Stephen F. Olford.*

Stephen F. Olford

Anyone who has seen Stephen Olford's library knows what an important part books have played in maturing his convictions. He names people and books that have generally influenced his life. First and foremost were his parents. Then there was the evangelist, Harold Wildish, whose impact on the island of Jamaica still lives on. His call to consecration and service, demonstrated in his life and communicated in his preaching, had a lasting effect on Stephen. Then there was Harold St. John, saint, scholar and able Bible teacher. Says Stephen: "To sit at his feet and hear the Word of God expounded, and to watch that same truth translated into Christian living, was something which convinced my young mind that Christianity really works." Another great influence was businessman A. Lindsay Glegg. Stephen adds, "His sanctified common sense and statesman-like advice over the years taught me much of the secret of balance and realism in the Christian ministry." There were others—Graham Scroggie, of course, and Capt. Godfrey Buxton, who was the founder and principal of the Missionary Training

Conclusion

Colony. His Bible readings every morning were rich, searching and practical. He was a man who manifestly lived what he taught. Then there was Dr. G. Campbell Morgan, Dr. W. E. Sangster, Professor James Stewart, and Dr. Martyn Lloyd-Jones.

In terms of books and written sermons there was a host of classic authors: John Owen, John Bunyan, John Calvin, C. H. Spurgeon, Handley C. G. Moule, Horatius Bonar, F. B. Meyer, Andrew Murray, Alexander Whyte and Alexander Maclaren. No wonder Stephen Olford's messages are so thoroughly sound in doctrine, so evangelical, so authoritative, so "God-conceived, Christ-centered and Spirit-controlled."

Another dimension was yet to be added. When the children of Israel came out of Egypt, they were first redeemed by the blood of the lamb. Then they crossed the Red Sea and, in type, were brought positionally through death and burial to resurrection ground. In the strength of that experience they could have gone on to conquer Canaan, but they failed to do so. Thus it was that, later, they had to cross Jordan. This was really a reconfirmation of the truth that they had already passed through death and burial to take their stand on the resurrection side of death. This second experience was made necessary because of their failure to make good on the first one.

A similar situation often arises with Christian believers. At conversion we are identified with Christ in His death, burial, and resurrection. We confess this truth publicly in water baptism. But like the children of Israel, many of us fail to make good in practice what we declare to be our position. As a result, some great crisis experience becomes necessary at a later stage in our spiritual pilgrimage. We experience what some call "a second blessing." It is not, of course, a new conversion. It is a new and more mature commitment to Jesus as Lord. It opens up Canaan. We enter into the rest, the resources, and the realities of all that we have in Christ. It is often accompanied by new power in the ministry.

When Stephen Olford dragged himself off his deathbed, dropped on his knees, and cried to God for mercy, longing for the Lord Jesus to be made real in his life, God met him. "For the first time in all those years," he says, "I experienced the realization of the glory and wonder of an indwelling Christ. I suddenly became aware that this broken, battered body of mine was a habitat, a dwelling place for the Son of God. And oh, the peace! Nobody told me. I didn't have a Bible open before me, but the wonder that this body of mine was the very dwelling place of the Son of God was so overwhelming that I just stayed there on my knees. Eventually I dragged myself onto my bed, and a wonderful peace came into my heart. Glory to God!"

He went, Elijah-like, in the strength of that heavenly food many days. In time there followed his tremendous ministry in Newport, South Wales, in the church, among young people, and above all, with the troops embarking for the front line in France. In the end he was drained and exhausted. As the war came to an end, he found himself emotionally depleted, physically ill, his vocal cords shot to pieces, and his soul spiritually dry. He wondered if he would ever preach again.

He says, "Somebody gave me a biography of D. L. Moody, and I read it through and it moved me profoundly. I read a biography of F. B. Meyer. One was an evangelist, one was a pastor, but their experience was just the same. I said: 'Lord, what did they have that I don't have, because I'm dry, absolutely dry?'

"I went into hibernation at a bed and breakfast flat, cancelled all my commitments, took two big suitcases of books, way back from the early writers and the Puritans—John Calvin, John Owen, Martin Luther—right up to Campbell Morgan, and modern books. *Veni Creator* by Handley Moule was a book that mightily moved me. So did A. J. Gordon's book on *The Ministry of the Spirit.* I had a little attic, all alone. I pored over those books day after day, hour after hour. At last I laid all the books aside, and I began to study Ephesians 5:18 on being filled with the Holy Spirit. I had a cross-reference in my Bible to 2 Corinthians 3:6, 17: 'The letter killeth, but the spirit giveth life. . . . Now the Lord is that Spirit: and where the Spirit of the Lord is, there is liberty.' This can be understood, where the Spirit is Lord—that is, where He is given His true deity and sovereignty—there is liberty! And God set me free!

"I went down and paid my bill. The lady asked, 'Is the food bad?' I said, 'No.' She then inquired, 'Why are you leaving?' I told her my story. She stood there with tears streaming down her face. She said, 'You talk like someone who came out of the Welsh revival.' 'Well,' I replied, 'God has revived my heart.' I picked up my books and I went into Cardiff. I remembered that on that very date I was supposed to preach at a big youth rally, but I had cancelled. A colleague of mine was preaching instead. I slipped into the meeting; I couldn't help it. I put my bags down and sat there. Then someone spotted me. When it was known I was there, I was called up to the platform. I said, 'No, I'm not going to preach!' I meant it. Finally I said, 'If you don't mind, I will tell the people what has just happened!' I gave my testimony. We were there until 2:00 A.M., leading souls to Christ."

That was just the beginning. From there Stephen Olford went to Hildenborough Hall. This was a conference center established by evangelist Tom Rees where hundreds of young people converged for holiday making and biblical teaching. Stephen spent the whole week sharing what he had learned from the Word of God concerning the work of the Holy Spirit in a believer's life— and there was revival.

[Olford relates:] "At the end of that week who should arrive from the United States but Torrey Johnson, Chuck Templeton, Billy Graham, Cliff Barrows, Stratton Shufelt and one or two others. As was the custom, there was a testimony meeting on the last night. Then to close the program, I preached on Ephesians 5:18. God came down in power. Tom Rees said, 'All who want dealings with God, who have not already come into blessing, go into the chapel. We are going to give Stephen Olford twenty minutes to rest.' I sat there with my head bowed.

"Suddenly I sensed a presence before me. I looked up and I saw this handsome, tall young man, Billy Graham. I can visualize him now in his light suit, sporting an impossible tie! He said, 'Why didn't you give an invitation?' I said, 'An invitation has been given. In twenty minutes I'll be meeting with all those who really want to know how to be filled with the Spirit. Why did you ask?' He said, 'I would have been the first to come forward. I don't know anything about this in my life.'

"He was unable to stay. He was going down to Wales. We made a date to meet in the Welsh town of Pontypridd, in Taff Vale, only eleven miles from my home, where Billy was having some meetings."

In the book *My Most Memorable Encounter with God*, Stephen recounts:

I found that Billy was seeking for more of God with all his heart; and he felt that I could help him. For most of

Conclusion

two days we were closeted at Pontypridd's hotel with our Bibles open, turning the pages as we studied passages and verses. The first day Billy learned more secrets of the "quiet time." The next, I expounded the fullness of the Holy Spirit in the life of a believer who is willing to bow daily and hourly to the sovereignty of Christ and to the authority of the Word. This lesson was so new to me that it cascaded out, revealing bright glimpses of the inexhaustible power of the love of God.

Billy drank it in so avidly that I scarcely realized the heights and depths that his spiritual life had reached already. At the close of the second day we prayed, like Jacob of old laying hold of God, and crying, "Lord, I will not let Thee go except Thou bless me," until we came to a place of rest and rejoicing. And Billy Graham said, "This is a turning point in my life; this will revolutionize my ministry."*

---

*Stephen F. Olford, "When the Spirit Became Lord" from *My Most Memorable Encounter with God,* David Enlow, ed. (Wheaton, Ill.: Tyndale House, 1977), 149-157. See also John Pollock's authorized biography, *Billy Graham* (New York: McGraw Hill, 1966), 38-39.

"Billy had been trying till then to preach to the Welsh people. His sermons didn't last for more than fifteen or twenty minutes. The biblically-literate Welshmen would say, 'That's a good introduction, but let's hear the sermon, man.'

"That night, however, it was different. It seemed as though God had brought people from everywhere. The church was packed. Billy preached on Belshazzar and, before he was anywhere near the end of the sermon, people were pouring out of the pews, kneeling, broken at the altar.

"I went home that night in my old Ford car. I woke my father up at two o'clock in the morning. He said, 'Where on earth have you been?' I said, 'Sit down.' At the kitchen table I told him the story. 'Dad,' I said, 'the world is going to hear from that young man!'"

In the strength of that second (or was it third?) blessing Stephen Olford has gone on ever since! It is at the heart of all he stands for as a believer. He sums it up like this: "While I believe I received the Holy Spirit at the time of my conversion as a young lad, I did not understand the meaning of the fullness of the Spirit until I was past twenty-one. Then I discovered it is possible for the Holy Spirit to be present without being president, to be dormant without being dominant. The Holy Spirit can be quenched and grieved in a believer's life. But when sin is exposed and self is executed, the Holy Spirit can fill to overflowing and anoint with authority and power. This experience I entered into after much agony of heart, study of the Scriptures, and appropriation by faith and obedience."

He adds: "The supreme discovery of my life has been that the Holy Spirit is in a believer's life; that the fullness and anointing of the Holy Spirit are not only blessings to be experienced, but imperatives to be obeyed. I found out that the Spirit-filled life is normal Christian living, and anything less is falling short of the glory of God and missing the mark. Moreover, to attempt to serve, either in prayer or in preaching, without the anointing of the Holy Spirit is to offer to the Almighty the fleshly efforts of Cain, instead of the spiritual sacrifices of Abel."[2]

LAST WORD FROM THE AUTHOR

To the glory of God, I now know that "there is no demand made on my life, which is not a demand on the life of Christ in me."

Conclusion

The Lord Jesus Christ is totally adequate. It is not Jesus plus; it is Jesus period! Everything is in Jesus, and Jesus is everything! We must go and tell a church of defeated Christians that there is *victory in Jesus!* The Highway of Holiness is mapped out for every one of us, and the signposts are clearly visible. Let us tread the pathway with disciplined obedience 'til we see our Savior face to face. Paul, the apostle, said it long ago: "As you have . . . received Christ Jesus the Lord, SO WALK IN HIM" (Col. 2:6).

NOTES

Introduction

1. Marvin R. Vincent, *Word Studies in the New Testament*, Vol. 3 (Grand Rapids: Eerdmans Publishing Co., 1957), 484.

Chapter One—The Issue of Sinfulness

1. Charles Colson, *The Body* (Waco, Tex.: Word Publishing, 1992), 304.

Chapter Three—The Issue of Holiness

1. The *Revised English Bible* renders this verse thus: "God called us to holiness, not to impurity."

Chapter Eight—The Issue of Alertness

1. Harold S. Martin, "Modern Idolatry," in *Pulpit Helps*, published by AMG International, Chattanooga, TN 37422 (May 1982), 10. Used by permission.
2. Joseph Harris, in *Sunday School Times*. Quoted in *Knight's Master Book of New Illustrations*, Walter B. Knight, ed. (Grand Rapids: Eerdmans Publishing Co., 1956), 605. Used by permission.
3. *Link and Visitor*. Quoted in *Knight's Master Book*, 489. Used by permission.

Conclusion

1. First published in 1952 by Eerdmans Publishing Co. Although out of print, it is a *must* for those who "hunger after righteousness." It is still to be found in Christian college libraries.
2. John Phillips, *Only One Life: The Biography of Stephen F. Olford* (Neptune, N.J.: Loizeaux Brothers, Inc., 1995), 35-40.

FOR FURTHER READING
AND RESEARCH

Arthur, Kay. *Cleansing and Filling: A Guide to Fellowship with God and a Life of Power in the Holy Spirit.* Chattanooga, Tenn.: Precept Ministries of Reach Out, Inc., 1991.

Barabas, Steven. *So Great Salvation: The History and Message of the Keswick Convention.* London: Marshall, Morgan & Scott, 1952.

Bonar, Horatius. *God's Way of Holiness.* Chicago: Moody Press, n.d.

Bonhoeffer, Dietrich. *The Cost of Discipleship,* rev. ed. New York: Macmillan, 1949.

Briscoe, Stuart. *The Fullness of Christ.* Grand Rapids: Zondervan Publishing House, 1965.

Dieter, Melvin E., Anthony A. Hoekema, Stanley M. Horton, J. Robertson McQuilkin, and John Walvoord. *Five Views on Sanctification.* Grand Rapids: Zondervan Publishing House, 1987.

Hopkins, Evan H. *The Law of Liberty in the Spiritual Life.* London: Marshall, Morgan & Scott, 1952.

Lawson, J. Gilchrist. *Deeper Experiences of Famous Christians.* Anderson, Ind.: The Warner Press, 1911.

Maxwell, L. E. *Abandoned to Christ.* Grand Rapids: Wm. B. Eerdmans Publishing Co., 1995.

_____. *Born Crucified.* Chicago: Moody Press, 1945.

For Further Reading and Research

_____. *Crowded to Christ*. Grand Rapids: Wm. B. Eerdmans Publishing Co., 1950.

McQuilkin, J. Robertson, gen. ed. *Free and Fulfilled*. Nashville: Thomas Nelson Publishers, 1997.

Meyer, F. B. *The Christ-Life for the Self-Life*. Chicago: Moody Press, n.d.

Olford, Stephen F. *Heart-Cry for Revival*. Memphis: EMI Books, 1987.

_____. *Not I, But Christ*. Wheaton, Ill.: Crossway Books, 1995.

_____. *The Secret of Soul-Winning*. Shippensburg, Penn.: Treasure House, 1994.

Paxson, Ruth. *Life on the Highest Plane: A Study of the Spiritual Nature and Needs of Man*. Chicago: Moody Press, 1928.

Pentecost, J. Dwight. *Pattern for Christian Maturity: Conduct and Conflict in the Christian Life*. Chicago: Moody Press, 1966.

Phillips, John. *Only One Life: The Biography of Stephen F. Olford*. Neptune, N.J.: Loizeaux Brothers, Inc., 1995.

Showers, Renald E. *The New Nature*. Neptune, N.J.: Loizeaux Brothers, Inc., 1986.

Stanley, Charles. *The Wonderful Spirit-Filled Life*. Nashville: Thomas Nelson Publishers, 1992.

Taylor, Howard and Geraldine. *Hudson Taylor's Spiritual Secret*. Ed., rev. Gregg Lewis. Grand Rapids: Discovery House Publishers, 1990.

Thomas, W. Ian. *The Saving Life of Christ*. Grand Rapids: Zondervan Publishing House, 1961.

Tozer, A. W. *The Divine Conquest*. Harrisburg, Penn.: Christian Publications, Inc., 1950.

_____. *The Pursuit of God.* London: Marshall, Morgan & Scott, 1948, 1961.

_____. *The Root of the Righteous.* Harrisburg, Penn.: Christian Publications, Inc., 1955.

STEPHEN OLFORD
CENTER FOR
BIBLICAL PREACHING

Our History

The Institute for Biblical Preaching was founded in 1980 to promote biblical preaching and practical training for pastors, evangelists, and lay leaders. After fifty years of pastoral and global ministry, Dr. Olford believes that the ultimate answer to the problems of every age is the anointed expository preaching of God's inerrant Word. Such preaching must be restored to the contemporary pulpit!

The Stephen Olford Center for Biblical Preaching was dedicated on June 4, 1988, in Memphis, Tennessee. It is the international headquarters for Encounter Ministries, Inc., and houses the Institute for Biblical Preaching.

Our Strategy

The purpose of the Institute for Biblical Preaching is to equip and encourage pastors and laymen in expository preaching and exemplary living, to the end that the church will be revived and the world will be reached with the saving Word of Christ. The program includes four basic activities:

☐ Institutes on expository preaching, pastoral leadership, essentials of evangelism, the fullness of the Holy Spirit, the reality of revival, and other related subjects.

☐ Workshops for pastors and laymen to preach "live" in order to have their sermons, skills, and styles critiqued constructively.

☐ 1-Day Video Institutes on Anointed Biblical Preaching hosted around the country for pastors and laymen who invite us.

☐ Consultations on pastoral and practical matters.

For further information write: Encounter Ministries, P. O. Box 757800, Memphis, TN 38175-7800; call (901) 757-7977; fax (901) 757-1372; E-mail, Olford@memphisonline.com; or visit our World Wide Web site: www.olford.org.

GENERAL
INDEX

General Index

General Index

SCRIPTURE INDEX

THE WAY OF HOLINESS

Signposts to Guide Us